Foreword 1

By The Secretary General IMO

The public, as well as others who use shipping services have the right to expect that the ship they board or which carries their cargoes is safe and, within the context of the voyage, seaworthy and otherwise fit for the purpose. Seafarers too have the right to expect that their ship is safe and that they will not be exposed to danger or unacceptably high levels of risk.

Adequate standards of safety and environmental protection exist in many companies but this, by itself, is not enough. Good safety management requires a commitment through all levels of a company's hierarchy and effective communication channels between the management ashore and those on board ship are a prerequisite of safe sea operations.

The International Code for the Safe Management of Ships and Pollution Prevention (the International Safety Management (ISM) Code, as it is widely known) aims at contributing to safer shipping and cleaner oceans by laying down requirements for a clear link between shore and sea staff of a company and for a designated person to strengthen that link. A key aspect of the ISM Code is that companies must have a verifiable safety management system in place. For the system to be effectively implemented there must be a commitment from the top, responsibilities assigned and measures in place to remedy deficiencies.

I believe strongly that the ISM Code represents a component of invaluable importance and significance in IMO's strive to improve safety at sea and preserve the marine environment from pollution by ships. It can only be implemented if everyone involved understands what they must do and extends the fullest co-operation to others who will be participating in the process. It may be, as is sometimes said, that the ISM Code is simply a restatement of good practices that have existed over the years, but for some it harbours many new elements that must be learned.

I trust that *Managing Safety and Quality in Shipping*, which makes a pioneering contribution to an evolving culture, will offer a significant contribution towards achieving the objectives of the ISM Code, thus enhancing maritime safety and the protection of the marine environment.

I therefore wish to congratulate warmly the author for the effort he put into writing such a valuable book and The Nautical Institute for its new initiative in sponsoring it.

William A O'Neil, Secretary-General
International Maritime Organisation

Foreword 2
By The President of BIMCO

As the world moves toward a global economy, so business must perform to more exacting standards. The shipping industry is in a way the first global industry. It is the link between nations and continents. The establishment of international cooperation and conventions has therefore a long history in the shipping industry.

The shipping industry has shown that free market forces can provide efficient cheap transport and it does this through a complex web of contracts and agreements. However, as ships increase in size, cargoes become more complex, and ferries run ever faster, the risks of disruption following an incident become correspondingly greater. Manufacturers drawn by the same economic forces need their goods just in time.

The public expects its oil to be delivered regularly and without incident and distributors require their outlets to be topped up on demand without the need to maintain costly stocks.

The shipping industry has no option but to offer a quality service at minimum price and to do this it has to be able to manage quality effectively.

The author of *Managing Safety and Quality in Shipping* argues that a shipping company can become more competitive only if it is able to offer safe and reliable service.

In this respect *Managing Safety and Quality in Shipping* provides the first comprehensive overview of the way modern management techniques can be applied in shipping to improve economic performance.

BIMCO, as spokesman for the shipowner, shipbroker and agent, has played its role in the quest for better safety management and quality. Great strides have been made. There is however need for improvement both at sea and ashore, in order to meet a more complex world.

In this foreword, I wish to emphasise that the mandatory nature of the ISM Code will ensure that no shipping company will be able to escape the process. ISM will accentuate the positive aspects of the Safety Management System and everyone in the company can benefit from the enhancement of safe

Southampton
SOLENT
University

MOUNTBATTEN LIBRARY
Tel: 023 8031 9249

Please return this book no later than the date stamped.
Loans may usually be renewed - in person, by phone,
or via the web OPAC. Failure to renew or return on time
may result in an accumulation of penalty points.

ISM•ISO 9002•TQM

A-M Chauvel

Published by The Nautical Institute
202 Lambeth Road, London SE1 7LQ, England
Telephone: 020 7928 1351

Typeset by Tradeset Ltd, Southall, Middlesex

Printed in England by O'Sullivan Printing Corporation, Southall, Middlesex

ISBN 1 870077 407

practices in ship operations. Reduced damage, improved safety consciousness, greater professionalism and improved morale are likely to bring genuine cost savings and better efficiency.

Every company in the industry will be effected by this important regulation on ship safety. This book by Mr A-M Chauvel has arrived just in time to provide the insight, concepts and techniques which will benefit owner, shipper and seafarer and consignee alike.

F Lorentzen, President, BIMCO

*To a believer, an optimist,
a good coach and more,
a real friend.*

*Thank you
Julian Parker*

A-M C

TEAM WORK CHARTER

The team meets regularly, to try to find practical solutions to problems identified by its members.

All members of the group are equal.

Each member in turn is entitled to express one idea at a time.

No other member should criticise an idea put forward by a member.

Respect for ideas expressed by a member begins by listening to them.

No energy should be wasted by focusing on the symptom.

The project must be defined clearly and everyone must understand its purpose.

A hasty conclusion may conceal a better solution.

Use of common methods and tools allows the team to advance in the same direction.

The success of the team is proportional to the participation of its members.

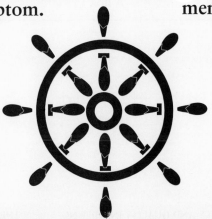

A key to analysing 'action' diagrams in this book

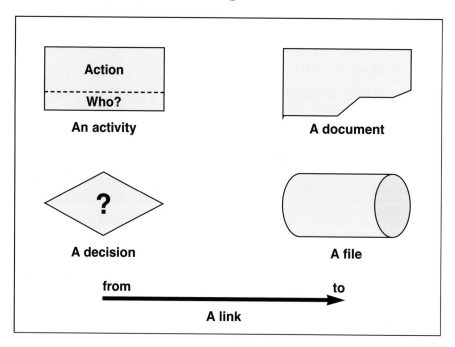

Contents

PART 1
Safety

Chapter 1
From Load Line to ISM certification

Introduction

It might seem strange that this book is entitled *Managing Safety and Quality in Shipping* particularly as a number of companies have already embraced the concepts of quality assurance and the ship management companies have introduced their own code of practice based upon similar principles.

It would of course be wrong to assume that the shipping industry did not have good safety control systems in place before the ISM Code became a statutory requirement. Many shipping companies successfully operate without accidents and have an impeccable safety record.

The reason for selecting safety first is based on the self-evident reflection that it is not possible to have a quality company which is not safe. Good safety management is the starting point for all commercial operations involving third parties.

Whether you come into this book at Part 1 for the ISM Code, Part 2 for quality assurance or Part 3 for total quality management is not important. Each of the parts is designed to stand alone or to be read as a continuous process.

To understand the need for the ISM Code it is first necessary to consider the evolution of safety systems in the shipping industry. The process of regulating shipping activity has evolved primarily in response to marine disasters like the *Titanic,* where loss of life was unacceptable. The explosions in crude oil carriers led to new methods of atmosphere control similarly the pollution of the marine environment following incidents like the *Torrey Canyon* foundering gave rise to a range of pollution control measuring. More recently the ro-ro ferry disasters of the *Herald of Free Enterprise* and the *Estonia* have led to new design rules and management practices.

The ISM Code, discussed in the first section of this book, is based on a new approach to safety. It sets out to provide a management system which will anticipate possible contingencies and, while giving recognition to the role of people, focuses on the unique characteristics of ships as marine vehicles and the need to protect the marine environment.

The purpose of a mandatory code is to stimulate and encourage the development of a safety based culture in the maritime sector.

Defining safety

Safety is a word which everybody understands but which is difficult to define. First, it is a relative concept deriving its meaning from a broad understanding of events out of which it is possible to say that activity 'a' is safer, or less safe, than activity 'b'.

Looking at it this way safety is a negative concept. It leads to the idea that accidents must be avoided. Paradoxically, because accidents cannot be predicted, this approach is very difficult to sustain in practice. In reality it is not possible, except in controlled situations where duplication and redundancy enable almost faultless operations, to have complete safety. Humans make mistakes and equipment, particularly at sea, can fail. Under these circumstances the aim is to anticipate what might cause an accident, and ensure that risks can be avoided before they become critical.

This is the concept behind safety management and the ISM Code Part 1. It is an enlightened step forward and, as can be seen in Parts 2 and 3, the same ideal can be applied to improve performance through quality, and to develop the effectiveness of the organisation through continuous improvement.

The evolution of safety concepts in shipping

To understand the present it is necessary to learn the lessons from the past. They are our only source of reference, based on real incidents which will enable us to move forward with the desire not to make the same mistakes again. Reflecting on past events gives rise to four levels of awareness:

▶ **Discovering:** associated with curiosity, wanting to know what went wrong and so leading towards better ideas for improvement.

▶ **Learning:** having discovered new and better ways of doing things, this knowledge has to be accepted and passed on to future generations and other colleagues in the industry.

▶ **Understanding:** once new ways of working have been established, research and reflection facilitate the level of understanding of principles based upon proven scientific methods.

▶ **Developing:** in the final stage of the cycle, based upon a deeper understanding, new systems can be developed with confidence because the outcome can be safely controlled.

The concept of freeboard
As long ago as the middle ages the Genoese marked their ships with a load line to prevent them being over loaded. This practical safety measure, to prevent the loss of the ship and its valuable cargo in bad weather, can be considered as *discovering* safety.

Today the Load Line Convention is a major influence on ship design and is one of the principal instruments through which ship's loading is regulated.

Safety of Life at Sea Convention (SOLAS)
A higher level awareness can be seen in the development of the Safety of Life at Sea Convention. Essentially people, and the safety of people, is the primary driving force behind rules for life saving and fire protection. The integrity of the ship and its systems are enhanced as people *learn* to provide equipment which can be used in the event of a disaster.

Marine Pollution Prevention Convention (Marpol)
Having considered the integrity of the ship and the well-being of the personnel on board, it was only logical to examine the impact on the marine environment of marine pollution. Above all it was felt that safeguards should be provided to prevent pollution incidents. This level of *understanding* is behind the Marpol Convention and its annexes.

Safety management (ISM Code)
Having prescribed requirements to ensure that ships are loaded properly; built and equipped to meet seagoing conditions; and are designed and operated in such a way that the environment will be protected, it becomes necessary to focus on the role of people and the human element so that at all times they can safely monitor and develop the management skills to improve ship operations.

This approach opens new horizons by accepting that the management of safety can be thought of as a system, just like production or processing. The purpose of the system has to be known; from this it is possible to decide if the safety limits are being over run. If they are, then corrective action must be applied and the process reviewed. This idea is fundamental to safe navigation, and its use in safety management systems is encapsulated in the ISM Code.

The main difference between navigation and the Code itself is that the Code covers the operation of the entire ship as part of a company. It enables all departments, the technical side and the operational side, to be integrated into one coherent system which is, of course, safer than operating isolated safety systems in specialised areas. Unless the integrity of the whole system is being managed, any error or omission may be undetected and lead to an accident.

The concept of risk

Risk is a concept closely associated with safety. When we say that something is 'risky' we mean that there is a good chance something may go wrong. In this way risk involves both the identification of the occurrence and the likelihood that it will happen. The dual nature of risk means that a dangerous situation, which happens rarely, can carry a risk similar to a safer activity which has to be carried out frequently.

Risk can thus be reduced by making events inherently less likely to fail or reducing the number of occasions when a hazardous event occurs. Safety can be dramatically improved by addressing both cause and frequency, and a good example of this was the introduction of routeing systems for ships.

The main problem was the uncertainty about what the other ship would do when meeting another nearly head-on. Like two pedestrians in a busy walk-way, they sometimes went to starboard only to find the other ship had gone to port, so engaging in what the experts call a dance of death.

The solution was to segregate all ships into lanes like a motorway, although at sea crossing is permitted. With this simple measure the 'end-on' encounter (the event) was prevented and the frequency reduced to zero.

Just when the ambassadors of safety advocate less risk, the business executive is being trained to take risks. Commercial competition demands that any new venture carries a risk of failure; similarly no organisation can stagnate for long without the risk of going into liquidation, or being taken over. Such are the realities of the market place.

Costing safety and assessing risks

The manager of any business enterprise has to assess the level of risk associated with each of the component parts of the company. In a shipping company these include: finance; commercial arrangements; personnel; ships; trades; operations and liabilities. If the risks are too high in any of these elements, the viability of the organisation itself may be put in jeopardy.

It is an unpalatable, but true, fact that in many companies safety is seen only as an additional cost. I am convinced the reason for this is the high level of legislation which is added each year and which companies have to absorb. How much will double hulls put on to the cost of a tanker? What is the cost of implementing the need for transverse bulkheads in ferries?

Such safety improvements have to be budgeted as a cost, as do new certification requirements for seafarers and the implementation of the ISM Code. Improved safety is thus seen by many in the industry as a penalty which is deducted from profits without a corresponding return. Not surprisingly many senior managers have a negative attitude to safety, born of experience.

Improving safety and reducing risks

Before any organisation can reduce its business and operational risks, it must have an effective system for monitoring its exposure and a way of dealing with contingencies. In the same way, if a shipping company wants to be attractive to clients, it must be able to provide an efficient and reliable service with the minimum of loss or damage to the cargo.

This leads to the concept of quality which relates to client satisfaction and their willingness to replace their business. This is the theme of Part 2. In Part 3 I explore the wider potential of joint ventures, based upon high levels of expectation which can be sustained over long periods through evolving client relationships.

However, before any of these higher levels of activity gain the confidence of clients, it is axiomatic that the parent company must be able to demonstrate that its operations are safe. What better way than to use the principles of the ISM Code?

Chapter 2
The concept of ISM

The concept of marine safety management is based on a structural and controlled approach similar to ISO 9000 standards relating to quality control systems.

Essentially the only major differences are:

The standard ISO 9002 covers the contractual concept of the relationship between a client and a supplier, and controls the quality of the expected service (see Part 2 – quality assurance); while

The ISM Code covers the organisation and provisions taken by the company to control safety and to prevent pollution risks.

All the aspects of the ISM Code may be grouped under four headings

■ Management

■ People

■ Ship and equipment

■ Procedures

As far as certification is concerned, these four aspects are subject to an assessment which leads to a document of compliance for the company, and a safety management ship certificate, attributable to each ship, renewable every five years and subject to periodical assessment.

Management
Company management is responsible for developing, implementing and maintaining an effective safety management system, onshore and on board its ships.

The aspects of the ISM Code that relate to management are:

▶ the development of company policy in relation to safety and the protection of the environment;

- the written definition of the responsibilities and authority of each person onshore and on board ship, with regard to safety and environmental policy. A designated person, acting directly for the general management of the company, must supervise implementation and maintenance of this policy;

- the preparation, distribution and periodic updating of a documentary system, in the form of procedures, plans and instructions. Accessible to all company personnel;

- the periodic review of the effective operation of the implemented system. This enables the identification of non-conformities followed by necessary corrective action to maintain a desirable level of safety on-shore and on the ship;

- the monitoring of the actions implemented in order to improve safety in the company, on the basis of actual experiences.

People

People are the key to the system. The human element is mentioned in 96 per cent of marine casualties, and 70 per cent of fires and explosions on board ship (figure 2.1, p10).

These figures do not indicate that the human element is the cause, but simply notes its presence at the time of the accident. It is one of many parameters but not necessarily the essential one.

The points of the ISM Code that relate to people are:

- qualifications because, with a reduced crew and increasingly sophisticated equipment, each action is important. Greater and recognised autonomy may be a question of survival for other members of the crew;

- communication between crew members because it is necessary to issue work orders without involuntary omissions, to ensure the continuity of safety and to avoid any fatal breakdown;

- provision of information to seafarers on their work and responsibility to carry out the master's wishes and crew tasks in a safe environment;

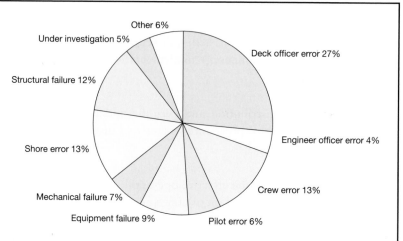

Human error is not, of course, limited to areas of direct action and there can be no doubt that many of the claims attributed to mechanical and structural failure have their real cause in lack of maintenance and proper care for the fabric and equipment on board ships, which is itself attributable to human failing. This failing may also occur at the design stage, the construction stage or indeed during periods of maintenance. It should not however be assumed that the human error is one for which culpability must automatically be attributable; a significant number of claims arise where there has been an error of judgment made by a responsible and careful individual. Nevertheless, even in these cases, there are often factors present such as fatigue, overwork or economic pressures which help to colour that judgment and may in themselves contribute to the human mistake.

Figure 2.1 Main causes of major claims (UK P&I Club)

■ training of crew and on-shore personnel to prevent errors and non-conformities which may be fatal at sea. This training also includes drills and exercises to simulate emergencies.

■ motivation of all personnel.

Ship and equipment

While the seafarer represents the behavioural element at the heart of the system, the ship and its equipment represents the 'hardware'.

It is essential to get the relationship between ship and seafarer right. It is vital for the seafarer to understand both his job and his working environment. People, the way they work, and the environment in which they work in must be taken in to account.

The essential points of the ISM Code referring to the ship and its equipment are:

- development of a preventative maintenance programme to minimise risks of breakdowns and accidents, but also to give the seafarer the possibility of controlling his work environment;

- identification and periodical inspection of all the equipment and systems considered as critical for the safe and effective operations of the ship;

- necessary inspection and control of instruments and materials which provide information on the operational condition of the ship. If operational and calibration procedures are drafted in the form of a programme, this will prevent omissions and will contribute to the creation of a safety-conscious environment for the whole crew.

Procedures

Procedures are not an end in themselves but a means of transmitting the expertise necessary in order to make progress. The essential reason for writing them down is to enrich them with acquired experiences but also to avoid recurring errors.

'Procedure' is the word most often used in the ISM Code. This shows the importance given to the change from an oral tradition to a written one. Speech will always be the carrier for daily activity. Written forms of expression are intended to record data essential to the proper functioning of the ship, and to ensure the exchange of information between the crews.

A new balance between oral and written traditions is being asked for. Good written documentation, and well drafted visual procedures, may become excellent tools for the training of personnel.

The essential points of the ISM Code relating to procedures are:

- drafting all the operational procedures for the ship to perform its mission, within the context of the company's policy for safety and environmental protection;

- preparation and maintenance of operational action plans which enable personnel to face and manage all foreseeable situations which may affect the safety of personnel or result in a pollution risk;

■ regular training of crews in emergency exercises and practices in order to prepare them for all eventualities;

■ systematic organisation of documented internal audits on the application of procedures recommended by the company, and the follow up of any corrective measures in line with the ISM Code.

■ analysis and handling of non-conformities observed during audits and controls.

There are two kinds of corrective action: **return** to the practice recommended by the procedure; or **modification** of the procedure if this improves the efficiency of the system;

■ recording of data and drafting necessary reports to document and demonstrate the effective operation of the system implemented by the company.

These written documents are the evidence required during assessment of the system implemented by the company by the external auditors.

Chapter 3
Understanding the ISM Code

Codes, standards, directives and other documents are not always written in a clear and simple language. This makes it hard to understand their essence and requirements on first reading. It is necessary to read and re-read them in order to discover the real requirements and implications for the company.

The purpose of this chapter is to understand the ISM Code (figure 3.1) taking the time needed to understand the essential points that will result in certification – currently essential for companies in the marine transport sector.

For practical reasons I shall not go into the minutiae of the Code since this depends on the activity of the company and its size. Implementation methods are set out in Chapter 4.

Objectives of the Code
The objectives of the Code are to guarantee safety at sea by preventing

---

ISM CODE REQUIREMENTS

2 - Safety & Environmental protection policy
3 - Company responsibilities & authority
4 - Designated person (s)
5 - Master's responsibilities & authority
6 - Resources & personnel
7 - Development of plans for shipboard operations
8 - Emergency preparedness
9 - Reports, non-conformities, accidents & hazardous occurrences
10 - Maintenance of ship & equipment
11 - Documentation
12 - Company verification, review & evaluation
13 - Certification, verification & control

Figure 3.1 ISM requirements

accidents and loss of human life, and to prevent risks of pollution in the marine environment.

The ISM Code should be read in this spirit and its implementation considered in the same light.

As with all system-based approaches, in order to succeed it is necessary to remain within the limits of the recommended system. Each time anyone strays, new interpretations result, which make the task harder for those who have to implement it.

Company objectives

The objective of the company in relation to safety should cover three points:

■ Providing operational practices in a safe working environment. The idea is to develop a programme oriented in the first place towards the personnel. Safety is for them; for their lives; and without their participation and contribution, the programme is worthless.

■ Establishing safety measures against all identified risks. This point is very important because it is realistic. The text reads 'against all identified risks' and not 'against all risks'. This is a crucial differentiation because absolute safety does not exist. Zero risk is not possible in this world.

The ISM text is clear: it requires each company, depending on the nature of its activities and experience, to identify these risks and take them into account in its improvement programme for safety and environmental protection:

■ Constantly improving staff skills, on shore and on board ship, in relation to safety management and preparation for all emergencies, in terms of safety as well as protection of the marine environment.

Success will be achieved progressively. It is based on changes in behaviour that cannot be ordered but depends on the conviction that these will achieve the desired result.

This effort must go beyond certification, bringing together seagoing and on-shore personnel, so the whole becomes one single system.

Practical means of implementation

The ISM Code is very well developed here. The company must develop and implement the system it has devised, and keep it up to date.

Although the text is innovative, compared with other codes and standards, the company should constantly read, develop, implement and improve the system it has devised.

A policy in relation to safety and the protection of the environment is the point of departure for this project. Without it, the project is doomed to fail. Drafted in an artificial way, and without real conviction, it may result in certification but has no chance of making the action undertaken last.

The policy for safety and environmental protection, just like any other, can only be drawn up by company management. If it is drafted by a safety or quality manager without the backing of senior management, it will never truly become the company's policy.

The company's personnel need to have a clear policy which demonstrates the commitment of its management so that they can, in turn, mobilise themselves around the action to be undertaken.

▶ Instructions and procedures to guarantee the safety of shipping operations and the protection of the environment. It is essential to study the procedures outlined.

▶ The procedures are obligatory because, without them, it is not possible to carry out an audit for the ship. Because they are so important, they form the subject of a documentary management process, formalised and defined by the company.

▶ The procedures lead to a documentary system. Linked to a procedure, the instructions permit the practical application of a part of the procedure to a work station. The issue of these instructions will be based on each situation encountered, according to the appraisal of the manager of the sector concerned. This point is important so as not to complicate the company's documentary management process.

▶ An established list of organisational responsibilities permit sea-based staff to communicate among themselves and with shore-based personnel.

▶ The Code demands clarification of the responsibilities and authority of each person, on-board and on shore, within the context of safety and protection of the environment; and also to establish lines of communication between each sector.

Only in this way can a coherent system be built around the theme developed by the Code. In order to succeed, the company must have one single policy, and responsibilities associated properly defined authorities.

Procedures in more detail

A **procedure** describes a specific activity and defines responsibilities and methods to attain an expected result.

An instruction is more specific and describes in sufficient detail a particular task to be accomplished inside a system in order for a specific requirement to be met.

The Code refers to the procedures documenting the system implemented. It does not specify the number of procedures to be drafted but it does specify the sectors which the procedures must cover.

These are as follows – and note that the numbers between brackets, eg (6.3) correspond to those of the ISM Code.

■ **Training** (6.3); to guarantee that new personnel and personnel appointed to new functions related to safety and the protection of the environment receive appropriate training;

■ **Information** (6.6); guaranteeing that the ship's personnel receive appropriate information on the safety management system in the language they understand;

■ **Programmes** for on-board operations (7.0); concerning the safety of the ship and pollution prevention;

■ **Emergency** situations (8.1); concerning the emergency situations likely to occur on board as well as measures to take in order to handle them;

■ **Notification** and analysis of non-conformities, accidents and hazardous occurrences (9.1); guaranteeing that non-conformities, accidents and hazardous occurrences are reported to the company, and that they are subject to an inquiry and analysis;

- **Corrective** actions (9.2); for the application of appropriate corrective and/or preventive measures.

- **Maintenance** of the ship and its equipment (10.1); to check whether the ship is maintained in a condition that conforms to the provisions of the relevant rules and regulations, as well as any supplementary instructions that might be drawn up by the company;

- **Identification** of equipment (10.3); permitting identification of technical equipment and systems that, if they were to break down, might be the cause of dangerous situations;

- **Documents** (11.1); permitting the control of all documents and information relating to the safety management system;

- **Internal audit** (12/12.3); the audits which should be carried out in accordance with established procedures.

Factors for success

The ISM Code is a reference document for the marine transport sector. It lists the requirements needed to achieve certification and recognition of the management system for safety and protection of the environment as implemented by the company.

- **Commitment:** Management commitment is the point of departure towards the policy it intends to implement. Without this commitment, nothing can result.

- **Skills:** today, in a world of international competition, we need skilled personnel at all levels of the organisation. This is a matter of survival.

- **Attitude:** The world and working relationships are constantly evolving. People have to learn to work as a team, considering everyone at each level as a partner rather than, say, a subordinate who simply has to obey orders.

- **Motivation:** A fascinating word, but often misunderstood. You cannot motivate personnel: you can only create an environment that is favourable to motivation. Any other consideration is illusory.

These four factors are highlighted because improvement of safety at sea rests on the human element. If you do not accept this idea, you cannot succeed in the development of shipping.

The following sub-sections, without necessarily covering all the points of the Code in detail, assist in understanding the official text. They should be complemented by the Code itself.

Safety and environmental policy

The ISM Code recommends that such a policy should be drafted by describing how the objectives will be realised. I believe this is an error because the Code is so new. It is clear that a policy is necessary – but we need a policy that can open doors towards progress, not focus only on short-term objectives.

The policy must provide an avenue, with an overall objective, where each person can find his place along selected priority axes, working towards managing a coherent activity.

The company's policy must be accompanied by an action plan specifying, for each year, the objectives to be reached.

These objectives must be both realistic and measurable. Positioning them over an annual period, they can be monitored and progress measured. If they extend for more than a year they become volatile, and the anticipated result may never be achieved.

Company's responsibilities and authority

The ISM Code recommends clear documentation of responsibilities and ensures that resources are adequate to cover all its requirements.

Very often it is easy to define the responsibilities of each person in the company; however the definition of authority is not so simple.

Today ships are operated by reduced crews, while the tasks to be accomplished remain the same. This means that each person has more to do to carry out the company's objectives. It is clear that this new approach requires better qualified staff. Levelling down of seafarers qualification can only lead to accidents that everyone will live to regret later.

If we want to succeed in implementing the ISM Code, not just for certification but for its own sake, it is necessary to define authority and agree the distribution of activity and power amongst the officers and crew.

> *Responsibility without authority*
> *is like a nail without a hammer.*

Designated person

The ISM Code recommends that one or more shore people have direct access to the highest level of management to guarantee safety in the operation of each ship.

This is an excellent idea but it is not practicable. Conflicts can be created if the same responsibility is given to two people. Instead of creating a unit there can be competition and conflict of interest.

One person only should be appointed to take charge of coordinating the programme. This person should be a member of the management committee, so that all decisions are ratified by the directors. The designated officer must have a direct relationship with top management so that his projections for resources and support are provided according to the needs of each ship.

There are areas where one has to be pragmatic: for example, if the head office is in Europe with a major operation based in the Pacific basin, it may make better sense for two people to liaise in getting the Code established.

Master's responsibilities and authority

The ISM Code recommends a precise written definition of the responsibilities and authority of the master on board ship. Within the context of the Code, these are:

■ To implement company policy, not his policy. This begins with explaining the policy and its roots to all the personnel sailing on the ships which he commands.

After this presentation, implementation of the policy continues with the application and conduct of the procedures in daily tasks.

■ To encourage the crew members to apply this policy through daily application of the procedures.

Certain working methods can be affected by new provisions. Resistance to change is a natural hindrance which must be overcome. The captain, supported by the first mate and the officers on board ship, should take the necessary time to train the personnel in the new procedures, and to ensure that everyone understands the changes made, and the reasons for these.

■ To give appropriate orders and instructions in a clear and simple fashion

The procedures document the safety management system on board ship. Even drafted in a clear and simple language, they are not always adequate and must be adapted to each specific situation.

If the procedures do not make sense to the crew, it is the responsibility of the master to issue more detailed instructions in order to adapt them to the level of comprehension of the personnel on board. Each time an instruction appears necessary for reasons of comprehension, the instruction issued must refer to the company procedure. The instruction is an additional item of information but never a substitute for the procedure.

■ To verify that the procedures and instructions are respected on board his ship.

This requires a control programme monitored by the master and delegated to the seagoing officers. This makes it possible to identify non-conformities in the system implemented, to look for causes, and to undertake the appropriate corrective actions. Without this activity, it is difficult, even impossible, to improve the safety management system on board ship.

■ To review the safety management system on board his ship and indicate the flaws to on-shore management

The ship is a unit in itself at command level. It is the master's responsibility to review the system in accordance with the methods specified by the company management. All this information, in relation to the fleet, enables management to carry out an overall review of the company safety management system.

Based on the analysis of this information, the company management will be able to define the the areas which need further attention for the maintenance of its policy.

Resources and personnel

The ISM Code recommends that all the personnel involved in the safety management system possess the qualifications required for the post occupied. But they must communicate in a working language that everyone understands and training must be given to all personnel concerned, depending on their requirements.

The company must first ensure that the master has the qualifications required for command. This includes a complete knowledge of the company's safety management system and the support necessary to perform his tasks with regard to safety.

When the command level on board ship is specified, it is necessary to ensure that each ship is allocated qualified seagoing personnel, physically able for the job. This is the responsibility of the company.

The new STCW Convention, revised in 1995, reinforces all the criteria for eligibility of seafarers and requires proof of the effectiveness of measures introduced to satisfy its intentions. The correction came into force in February 1997.

As far as newly appointed seagoing personnel, or personnel assigned to a new post relating to safety and protection of the environment, are concerned, it is necessary to provide familiarisation training and issue them with the written documents with which they must be familiar before sailing. For on-shore personnel, it is also necessary to provide for training when the post is an integral part of the safety management system of the company.

This training is especially important, since the interface between the seagoing and on-shore personnel is often the weak link in the system.

Training is essential, since the effectiveness of the system relies on the skills of the personnel ready to deal with any eventuality and act with efficiency.

The Nautical Institute, in its book on maritime education and training, points out that, to most people, seafaring is an unnatural way of life. The ways of the sea, living on board, and current use of powerful equipment have to be learnt and it is important to ensure that training levels are appropriate to the needs of seafarers.

The important problem to be resolved is that of the working language on board ship. The ideal is one single language, of course. Since the reality is anything but, provisions must be taken so that the communication necessary to effective operations of the system is not a Tower of Babel. Without an effort in this respect, training and procedures will not be as effective as hoped, and prevention will only be a pious wish.

It is at this level that instructions, without ever replacing oral communication as such, may find their legitimate place as a means of understanding the expected tasks. They should also be drafted in one language or in a visual form adapted to the reader for whom they are intended. Communicating is an art which cannot be improvised.

Development of plans for shipboard operations

The ISM Code recommends the drafting of procedures and instructions for the main operations on board ship concerning the safety of the ship and the prevention of risks of pollution.

A plan is a document which sets out the operating methods, the resources and the sequence of activities linked to the subject. This is a coherent whole: (eg: emergency plan, training plan, control plan etc).

An instruction is specific to a work station. It describes in detail what must be done here in order to ensure maintenance of the effective operation of the system. It is a specific element, such as oiling of the engine, launching of lifeboats etc.

Whatever the nature of the document, it is necessary to identity the action to be carried out and to be able to find in this document the responses to the following questions:

> *What, who, when, where, how and why?*

The objective is to make available to the personnel all the information they need so that they can carry out their jobs in a set of coherent activities.

Emergency preparedness

The ISM Code recommends the identification and description of the emergency situations likely to occur on board the ship, but also the measures taken to deal with them, including the development of a programme of appropriate exercises. All shipping companies are now required to have an appropriate emergency response capability.

The ISM Code, in relation to this chapter, puts the emphasis on the prevention of risks on board ship. Prevention is better than cure. The notion of a programme covers the procedures, plans and instructions relating to these situations.

Theoretical training is the initial point of departure, but it does not permit the identification of gaps and real training needs for personnel to be ready to handle these situations.

Only by putting yourself in the situation can you check the capability of the crew to react in time and identify the real training needs (see figure below). Repetition of emergency exercises is indispensable because, however well the programme is designed, without constant practice it is soon forgotten. Only 20 per cent of theoretical learning is remembered. During real situation practices, this may exceed 70 per cent.

EXERCISE SCHEDULE — Week

	1	2	3	4	5	6	7	8	9	10	11
Oil and chemical spillage	X										
Colision / salvage		X									
Fire on deck				X							
Fire engine room							X				
Fire lower voids			X								
Galley fire											
Fire restaurant / main hall					X						
Man overboard						X					
Bomb threat explosion											
Hazardous									X		
Blackout											X
Helio operation								X			
Structural failure										X	
Evacuation and abandonment											

Figure 3.2 Exercise schedule

Reports and analysis of non-conformities, accidents and hazardous occurrences

The ISM Code recommends that this information is passed on to the company and is the subject of enquiries, analyses and appropriate corrective and/or preventive actions.

This is another delicate point. In fact, while this subject seems necessary in order to create constructive responses aimed at the continued improvement of safety, its implementation can only succeed if people are prepared to accept it. What master is prepared, these days, to report all this information, if it would result in blame and questioning of his professional capacity?

In any enquiry into a system, the object is not to identify who is at fault but to understand why the system implemented is failing. Based on the analysis of the problem, it then becomes possible to understand the reasons for, and to make the system evolve to prevent repetitions (figure below).

Safety is not a matter for procedures. These are there so that history is not forgotten, to transmit an expertise which is evolving, and to make sure the same errors are not repeated by forgetting this expertise.

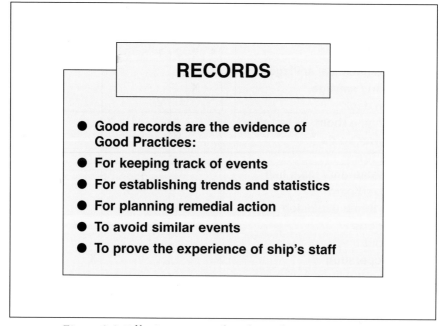

Figure 3.3 Effective action plan depends on good records

Safety is a matter for all personnel, whatever their job. It is necessary to train them, listen to them and take account of each idea as a step towards improving procedures, and therefore safety on board ship.

Maintenance of the ship and its equipment

The ISM Code recommends examination of the ship and its equipment through inspections and making sure appropriate corrective actions are taken.

After thinking about personnel and the safety system, it is time to talk about the condition of the ship and its equipment. A good worker without a good tool cannot do good work. This is a truth which goes back to the beginning of time.

Even if the ship is subject to classification and statutory visits, all these supervisory operations are not the subject of an overall assessment of risks. Each inspection is a one-off. It only covers, at one time, part of the technical elements linked to safety.

This approach should be complemented by an internal programme of maintenance on board ship. The maintenance management programme

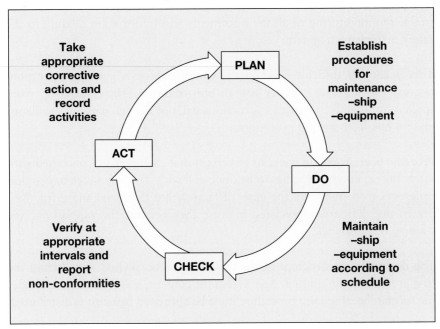

Figure 3.4 Internal programme for preventive maintenance.

should be based on the principle; plan, do, check, and act.

- **Plan:** preparing a programme for the maintenance and control of equipment and materials having a direct impact on the effective operation of the ship;

- **Do:** carrying out the plan according to the planned schedule. Anomalies should be recorded and be the subject of corrective actions;

- **Check:** by internal inspections according to the planned schedule. Once again, any anomaly in the application of the programme should be noted and be the subject of corrective actions on a system level;

- **Act:** taking the necessary measures in relation to the ship, but also reporting the difficulties encountered with the personnel on shore in order to keep the system operational. Once again the object is not to find someone responsible but rather to find solutions to improve safety on board ship. This is a change in approach which requires time and patience.

Documentation

The ISM Code recommends the drafting and maintenance of procedures to enable the monitoring of all the documents and information relating to the safety management system.

This is another difficult point in the Code when it is put into operation, because the shipping industry has an oral tradition. The changeover from spoken commands to written instructions will not happen without problems; and no one likes writing procedures.

Procedures are useful in order to be certain that each person, concerned with safety at sea, knows what has to be done and why. They are necessary so that progress can be made on the basis of facts rather than trial and error. Well drawn up, they are appreciated because they become the support for the training of personnel.

The documentary structure of the system must be devised even before the first procedures are drafted. Apart from the content, it is essential to consider the format, because each procedure must be approved before it is distributed.

Distribution of these documents must be controlled so that any modifications may be sent to the relevant parties, and to ensure that any outdated document is rapidly withdrawn from the system.

Without these precautions, management of the documentary system is impossible and the effectiveness of the system suffers.

Company verification, review and evaluation

The ISM Code recommends internal audits at system level, but also a periodic assessment of the effectiveness of the system to ensure its development.

An internal audit is not a control: Importantly:

■ **The purpose of a control** is to note deviations from a technical reference. Responses are two-fold, conforming or not conforming to the specification;

■ **The purpose of the internal audit,** in relation to a system, is to understand the deviations observed and to recommend what is best for the company, within the context of the requirements of the code;

The recommendation may lead to the following decisions:

▶ reinforcement of application of the procedure, because it is necessary in its current form;

▶ modifications of the procedure, so that it can evolve on the basis of the practices observed;

▶ modification of the procedure, to avoid a new type of risk not currently taken into account by the procedure.

The internal audit must never be a surprise for the manager of the audited sector, or the personnel. The purpose of the internal audit must be specified before it is carried out, and the sector manager kept informed of the date and its purpose.

For the audit to bear fruit, it is important that the sector manager concerned can take any necessary corrective action to remedy the non-conformities reported without delay.

Certification, verification and control

The ISM Code recommends that a certificate, subject to checks and controls, is issued to any company and any ship which satisfies the specifications of the ISM Code.

For the company, the certificate is a document certifying compliance with the requirements of the ISM Code; for the ship, the certificate is a safety management certificate.

The safety management certificate, allocated to the ship, can only be issued if the company already possesses a document certifying compliance for its operations on shore.

Certification of the safety management system is developed further in the next chapter.

Chapter 4
How to implement ISM

The ISM Code is formulated in general terms so that it can be widely applied. In chapter 3, we concentrated on understanding the Code, to understand principles before putting it into practice. The purpose of this chapter is to describe its implementation, step by step.

The method proposed takes accounts of the requirements of the Code along with management elements of the programme.

The 10 steps in this programme are:

1 Initial assessment
2 Strategic planning
3 Safety and environmental protection policy
4 Responsibilities and authority
5 Project team
6 Company procedures
7 Shipboard procedures
8 Measurement and reporting
9 Personnel training
10 Final assessment
11 Certification

The word 'procedure' appears twice in the steps of the programme, for two reasons:

▶ First, it is the key word most frequently mentioned in the Code. This clearly demonstrates the importance of procedures in the documentary system which must be created by the company;

▶ Second, the procedures necessary on shore and on board a ship are not the same. They are specific to each ship, depending on the tasks carried out by the ship, and additional to the company procedures.

Apart from this, the other steps concern management practices for the programme. Each is presented in an identical way.

The figure 4.1 (p30) presents the general schedule for implementation of the ISM Code.

HOW TO IMPLEMENT ISM CODE	2 - Safety and Environmental protection policy	3 - Company repsonsibilities & authority	4 - Designated person(s)	5 - Master's responsibilities and authority	6 - Resources and personnel	7 - Development of plans for shipboard operations	8 - Emergency prepardness	9 - Reports, non-conformities, accidents and hazard, occur	10 - Maintenance of ship and equipment	11 - Documents	12 - Company verification, review and evaluation
Initial assessment	1										
Strategic planning	2										
Safety & Env. prot. policy	┗►	3									
Responsibilities & authority		┗►	4	5		7					
Project team					6						
Company procedures						┗►	8	9	10	11	12
Shipboard procedures							8	9	10	11	12
Measurement & reporting										┗►	13
Personnel training					14 ◄						
Final assessment	15 ◄										

Figure 4.1 The schedule for the implementation of the ISM Code

1 Initial assessment

Objective: Define the required performance on shore and on board ship, in relation to the system, in order to conform to the ISM Code. This first step consists of:

► evaluating the current practices of the company in relation to the requirements of the Code;

► identifying the deviations in relation to each chapter of the Code;

► presenting the deviating observed to the company's general management, and the sectors where improvements are desirable to obtain ISM certification.

The initial assessment relates to all the activities on shore and on board the ships concerned by certification. During this assessment, not all ships are seen, but at least one ship per specific activity, so the assessment can indicate any weaknesses in the current system. The results of the initial assessment should be used as a reference to measure progress as the project is realised.

This step may be regarded as a snapshot of the safety management system currently in place in the company.

The initial assessment requires the participation of each company manager. This is a project based on team work, even if the task is assigned to someone outside the company. The working plan is the same for certification:

Review of the documentary system

Audit of the practices on shore and onboard several ships.

Each manager must list supportive documentary evidence used in his department or on board his ship, and indicate existing gaps in these. This assessment is even more important since it shapes the action plan for obtaining the certification necessary to ships, so that they can continue to carry out their tasks without breaking any regulations.

The initial review of the system is carried out according to the following model (figure 4.2 below):

0 per cent: No evidence of written procedures.

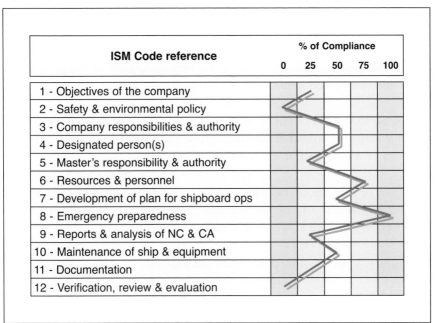

ISM Code reference	% of Compliance				
	0	25	50	75	100
1 - Objectives of the company					
2 - Safety & environmental policy					
3 - Company responsibilities & authority					
4 - Designated person(s)					
5 - Master's responsibility & authority					
6 - Resources & personnel					
7 - Development of plan for shipboard ops					
8 - Emergency preparedness					
9 - Reports & analysis of NC & CA					
10 - Maintenance of ship & equipment					
11 - Documentation					
12 - Verification, review & evaluation					

Figure 4.2 The initial review of the safety management system

25 per cent: Existence of written procedures covering part of the requirements of the Code.

50 per cent: All the procedures are written and adequately cover the requirements of the Code.

75 per cent: The personnel is aware of the existence of the procedures. The procedures have been the subject of training.

100 per cent: An audit confirms that the procedures are being enforced.

2 Strategic planning

Objective: Achieve implementation of the ISM Code at shore-based centers and on board ships, in due time and at reasonable cost.

Based on the deviations observed during the initial assessment, a programme must be prepared with the aim of obtaining ISM Code certification within an acceptable period of time. This second step consists of:

▶ creating the action plans, sequence by sequence, on shore and on board the ships

▶ defining and selecting realistic dates for each action

▶ identifying the resources required for implementation of the programme within the agreed periods.

Following the report obtained from the initial assessment, it is necessary to plan the action to be undertaken in the time given. Implementation may take between 16 and 24 months.

A project of this size cannot be carried out blindly. The plan has an impact on the motivation of the participants. Sometimes it is necessary to be reminded of the three elements that form the objective:

▶ realistic in terms of methods and time allowed

▶ measurable in terms of comparison

▶ controllable in terms of responsibility

If the company resources are insufficient, it should use external skills.

Not all of the points of passage proposed below have to be taken into consideration, but the fact of asking these questions may avoid forgetting something important.

Initial assessment of the system

operational planning at head office, onshore centres and standard ships
documentary review of the existing system at head office
audit of the on shorebased system
audit of the system on board the ships selected
preparation of the assessment report
presentation of the report to the company management

Strategic planning

management seminar on the ISM Code
definition of priorities trends and objectives
preparation of the action plan
approval of the action plan

Safety and environmental protection policy

development of the policy draft
final review of policy
commitment of general management
formalisation of the policy
internal/external communication plan
presentation to personnel
implementation

Responsibilities and authority

company flowcharts
definition of responsibilities, authority and operational links
head office and on shorebased centres
designated person(s)
master and officers on board ship

Project team

definition of the task
selection of members
definition of responsibilities, authority and operational links
training in project and team work
providing information to personnel
launching of the project

Company procedures

development of the documentary structure
detailed review of existing procedures
identification of documentary requirements
planning of the preparation of documents
drafting of documents
approval of documents
publishing of documents
implementation of documents.

Shipboard procedures

identification of the requirements specific to each type of ship
development of the documentary structure specific to each ship
detailed review of existing procedures
implementation of documentary requirements
planning and preparation of documents
drafting documents
approval of documents
publishing of documents
implementing documents

Measurement and reporting

content, form and frequency of report
responsibility for preparation
role of general management

Personnel training

identification of requirements

preparation of the training programme
approval of the training programme
training management
training personnel
internal auditors
appraisal of training courses

Final assessment

planning the audits
designation of the audits
realisation of the audits
presentation of the report to the general management of the company
implementation of corrective actions, if necessary
preparation of the certification request file

The initial strategic planning will probably be reviewed, after several months, to become more realistic. The advantage is in having prepared it, and knowing what is to be modified, and why will determine impact on the expected result.

3 Safety and environmental protection policy

Objective: make all the aware of the company policy selected and the commitment of the management to ensure the success of the project.

At this stage the company has a programme for implementing the ISM Code on shore and on board ship. The project must be legitimised. The third step consists of:

▶ drafting the company's safety and environment protection policy

▶ informing all of the personnel of the importance of the project for the company, of its content and the planned process of implementation

▶ communicating the safety and environmental protection policy and also explaining it point by point, so that everyone can understand how they are directly affected by its implementation.

By informing all the personnel before launching the programme, the management shows its commitment to the project and its determination for it to succeed in the time allocated.

Safety & Environmental Protection Policy

Our success rests essentially on the skill of our staff.

We must offer each employee, on shore and on board ship, a danger free working environment, and give him the means to improve his skills.

Faced with the growing market demand and in order to respect the environment, we must draft and implement the necessary provisions to prevent any risk of accident and pollution, and to be able to respond at any time to any emergency situation.

The success of our company over time is seen as a continuous progress

We must develop a performance programme for the improvement of safety for our personnel and for the protection of the environment, with the participation of all the levels of our organisation.

In the name of our company, I make a personal commitment to this policy, which is vital for our future, and I count on your participation.

It is also necessary to remember that safety and environmental protection policy is one of the requirements of the ISM Code. This is the keystone of the programme and the first commitment of the project. It can only be devised and drafted by the general management of the company. If drafted by the safety manager alone, it risks being seen as his policy and not that of the company.

■ A good policy must be:

▶ sufficiently wide reaching to resist the erosion of time, so that each person can find improvement projects within it

▶ oriented towards the human element, so that this can be identified in the company policy

▶ comprehensible to everyone, showing the goal to be achieved

▶ show the unconditional commitment of the general management

4 Responsibilities and authority

Objective: to ensure that everyone concerned in the certification project knows what management expects from them.

When the policy is drafted, it is vital to define the role of everyone to implement and maintain the policy over time. This fourth step consists of:

▶ defining responsibilities and authority at all levels of the organisation

▶ establishing operational links, as clearly and as simply as possible, between company departments

▶ documenting the responsibilities and authority of the departments and the operational links between the departments.

These documents are part of the company's safety and environmental protection manual. They must be present permanently in the on shorebased centres and on the ships.

Responsibilities and authority are part of a process of delegation based on the objectives to be reached. Apart from responsibility for the action and the authority on the action, delegation relates to the skills of the function and responsibility for its result.

Responsibilities and authority for each function must be drafted clearly and concisely. They must not form a succession of interminable litanies which are never understood and difficult to update. The company flowchart is the point of departure to clarify who does what, and who is responsible for what. Each function can only have one responsible.

5 Project team

Purpose: develop and carry out all necessary actions within the context of the selected programme, and to resolve any problems which may have adverse consequences on the success of the project.

In order to succeed, the company management must be involved in the project: but it is also necessary to rely on a team which is responsible for carrying it out. This fifth step consists of:

▶ appointing the members of the team charged with concluding the project

▶ designating the project manager who coordinates all the activities necessary to achieving the objective

▶ defining the responsibilities of each member within the team charged with the project

▶ carrying out the actions according to the programme and the responsibilities allocated to each member of the team.

The project manager should report directly to the company manager in relation to this project. The team members coordinate all necessary activities in their sector of competence.

Implementation of activities is the responsibility of each manager within his department. The person designated under the safety and environmental protection policy should also assume coordination of the project.

It is not necessary to create another level of responsibility that will only hinder the project.

The team should be made up of people who already have management responsibilities within the company, because once the project is concluded, they will have to continue to assume responsibility for maintenance of the policy within their department. The elementary process for realisation of the project is as follows:

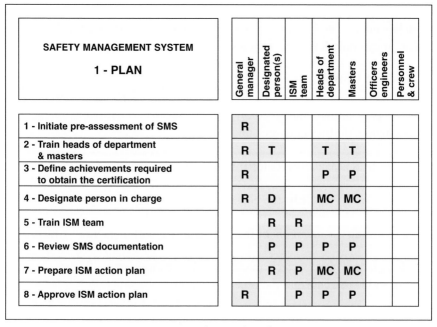

SAFETY MANAGEMENT SYSTEM 1 - PLAN	General manager	Designated person(s)	ISM team	Heads of department	Masters	Officers engineers	Personnel & crew
1 - Initiate pre-assessment of SMS	R						
2 - Train heads of department & masters	R	T		T	T		
3 - Define achievements required to obtain the certification	R			P	P		
4 - Designate person in charge	R	D		MC	MC		
5 - Train ISM team		R	R				
6 - Review SMS documentation		P	P	P	P		
7 - Prepare ISM action plan		R	P	MC	MC		
8 - Approve ISM action plan	R		P	P	P		

Figure 4.3 Defining the objectives

SAFETY MANAGEMENT SYSTEM 2 - DO	General manager	Designated person(s)	ISM team	Heads of department	Masters	Officers engineers	Personnel & crew
1 - Prepare S&EP policy and company commitment	R	P					
2 - Inform personnel on project			MC	R1	R2	I	I
3 - Assign responsibilities ashore and on board ship	I	P		R1	R2	I	
4 - Implement SMS ashore		P	R				
5 - Train personnel ashore and officers		R	P	P	P	T	T
6 - Implement SMS on board ship		P			R	P	
7 - Train crews on board ship					R	D	T
8 - Co-ordinate ISM action plan	I	R	P	I	I		

Figure 4.4 Implementing the system

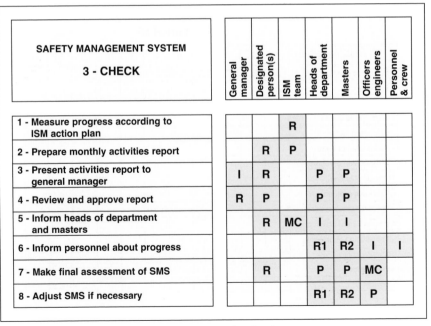

SAFETY MANAGEMENT SYSTEM 3 - CHECK	General manager	Designated person(s)	ISM team	Heads of department	Masters	Officers engineers	Personnel & crew
1 - Measure progress according to ISM action plan			R				
2 - Prepare monthly activities report		R	P				
3 - Present activities report to general manager	I	R		P	P		
4 - Review and approve report	R	P		P	P		
5 - Inform heads of department and masters		R	MC	I	I		
6 - Inform personnel about progress				R1	R2	I	I
7 - Make final assessment of SMS		R		P	P	MC	
8 - Adjust SMS if necessary				R1	R2	P	

Figure 4.5 Carrying out the final assessment

SAFETY MANAGEMENT SYSTEM 4 - ACT	General manager	Designated person(s)	ISM team	Heads of department	Masters	Officers engineers	Personnel & crew
1 - Prepare schedule for certification	I	R	I	P	P		
2 - Prepare file for certification		R	P	I	I		
3 - Obtain Document of Compliance for shorebased operation		R	I	P			
4 - Obtain Safety Management Certificate for ships		R	I		P		
5 - Inform personnel on obtaining the certificates	R	I	I	I	I	I	I
6 - Recognise people for outstanding efforts and contributions	R	P		P	P		
7 - Prepare safety improvement plan for the coming year	R	R	MC	P	P		
8 - Plan date for SMS review	I	R	I	I	I		

Figure 4.6 Obtaining certification

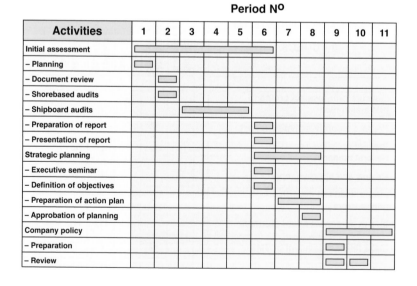

Figure 4.7 Following the progress

- **define achievement**

- **implement SMS**

- **make final assessment**

- **obtain SMS certification**

▶ Each step of the process must clearly identify the sequence of actions to be undertaken and the consequent responsibilities.

By way of example, figures 4.3, 4.4, 4.5, 4.6 and 4.7 show the sequence of actions to be taken and the responsibilities for each stage of implementation of the action plan.

Where: R = Responsibility   R1 = on shore based   R2 = on board ship
P = Participation
I = For information
MC = May contribute
T = Training required

Each company, depending on its organisational structure, should define its own process within the context of its project.

6 Company procedures

Objective: describe as clearly as possible all of the activities which contribute to maintenance of the safety and environmental protection policy of the company.

The first activities to undertake are generally in relation to the on shorebased centres, in order to manage the ISM system Code. This sixth step consists of:

▶ listing the existing documentary system in each sector of the company

▶ analysing each existing procedure in terms of conformity to the ISM Code

▶ identifying any elements missing from the system

▶ draft missing or obsolete procedures

▶ create the company's documentary system in accordance with the requirements of the Code

Responsibility for the system documentation (procedures, instructions and other documents) should fall on each department manager.

All the documentation necessary to conform to the requirements of the ISM Code makes up the 'safety and protection of the environment' procedures manual. The procedures constitute the backbone of the documentary system. Without these it would not be possible to carry out an audit of the system implemented by the company.

Reflection on the structure of the documentary system is essential because there are no formal rules. Depending on the size of the company, it may be preferable to have one single manual including all of the procedures, or to create several manuals.

Whatever model is used, the procedures must be written in the working language of the personnel. They must be drafted clearly and concisely.

The documentary system relies on a classic current model:

▶ policies and responsibilities
▶ general procedures for on shore-based operations, common to all ships
▶ procedures specific to a type of ship
▶ work instructions when necessary

7 Shipboard procedures

Objective: describe as clearly and simply as possible all specific activities necessary on each ship and their interfaces with on shore-based centres, to ensure maintenance of the company policy wherever the ship is located.

As the documentary system is created onshore, it is necessary to think about the direct implications and the necessary interfaces with the ships for the system to become operational. This seventh step consists of:

▶ listing the documentary system existing on board each type of ship

▶ analysing each existing procedure in terms of its conformity with th requirements of the ISM Code

▶ identifying the elements missing for each ship

▶ drafting any missing or obsolete procedures

▶ creating the documentary system for each ship in accordance with the on-shore documentary system and in relation to the requirements of the ISM Code.

Responsibility for system documentation (procedures, instructions and other documents), should call to each departmental manager.

There is only one policy, that of the company. This is the same on shore and on board ship.

The sections constituting the policies manual, the general procedures manual and the procedures specific to the ship concerned should be available on board each ship. All this documentation required by the ISM Code constitutes the safety and environmental protection manual specific to the ship.

Even when well drafted, a procedure may not be sufficient in itself especially in the case of multinational crews. It may then be necessary to have recourse to work instructions specific to several posts on board the ship. This responsibility falls to the master and his officers.

A work instruction is the application of part of a procedure. If it has to be translated into work instructions, there may be a problem with drafting. Instructions must never become permanent substitutes for gaps in the way people responsible have drafted the procedures. They are aids and not obligations.

A work instruction may be a drawing, numbered pictograms or a simple text of stages to follow, drafted in the spirit of the procedure.

All procedures, for the company and its ships, are part of the documentary system which permits demonstration of the effectiveness of the company policy in relation to the requirements of the ISM Code.

8 Measurement and reporting

Objective: Enable the general management of the company to follow the progress of the project and to act when the situation requires this.

The time required for complete implementation of the system depends on a number of criteria (size of the company, nature and number of ships, available internal resources etc.). It may be several months before the objective is reached.

Preocuppied by daily activities, the parties involved in the project may put off the measures undertaken and the time frame will never be adhered to. This eighth step consists of:

▶ drafting, at the beginning of the programme, a schedule of meetings to review the progress of the project

▶ creating a system for monitoring the project, placed directly under the responsibility of the project manager

▶ identifying the deviations and their causes

▶ taking necessary corrective actions in order to keep to the time scales or, as a last resort, modifying the programme of activities.

The presence and direct involvement of the general management of the company during these meetings is essential. It confirms its wish to see the programme succeed and contributes to the motivation of the team charged with concluding the programme. Formalising the monitoring of the project is not a luxury but simply good management practice.

The certification process should not be perceived as an expense because it is becoming compulsory. It must be considered as an investment, the return from which does not depend solely on the initial expenditure, but on research into the efficiency of the actions undertaken. As stated earlier, it is necessary to define at the beginning of the programme the content but also the form and the frequency of reports and reviews.

During these reviews it will be possible to modify the programme, if the situation demands, taking account of the impact of these decisions. In the case of delay, the important thing is to understand the reason and to take all necessary measures to maintain the final objectives.

9 Personnel training

Objective: develop and improve the skills of personnel on shore and on board ships with regard to application of the company policy relating to safety and protection of the environment.

Even the most complete documentary system only has a chance of obtaining a concrete result if the personnel alone has access to the information. It must also understand and contain this information. This ninth step consists of:

- preparing a cycle of training for all the managers involved in the implementation of the new system

- setting up the mechanisms and the means to multiply awareness of the system implemented on shore as well as on the ships

- arrange for the training of new employees in order to keep the system operational

- arrange for necessary training when modifications are made to the system

- train the personnel according to the training cycle selected

It is not necessary to create a training manual. The best manual for management and personnel is the procedures manual if it has been properly drafted. Video cassettes may cover specific technical aspects. Imagination is required to maintain the level of personnel skills.

Procedures are the first support to use during training. A simple principle exists: a procedure without training is a useless document. Training is an integral part of the implementation of a procedure. It is necessary to specify at each publication of a procedure the training of those who are concerned with its daily implementation.

Training in procedures must be accompanied with practical exercises, in particular for emergency situations. It should be carried out in cascades, by the managers responsible for the sectors concerned, and be the subject of an appraisal. The training programme may include:

- familiarisation with the ISM Code
- implementation of the ISM Code
- drafting procedures
- internal audit
- problem solving etc.

The form depends on the experiences already acquired by the company and the equipment it possesses on shore and on board ships: formal courses, syndicate work session, individual training, using material and equipment such as videocassettes, slides, overhead transparencies or exercises.

Training should be a continuous process aiming to improve personnel skills, and to integrate new employees into the operating teams (Figure 3.13).

10 Final assessment

Objective: prove that the system implemented will enable the company to obtain ISM Code certification.

This is the culmination of the project for certification of the system in relation to the requirements of the Code. Between the initial assessment and this step, several months will have passed with highs and lows. Is the company finally ready for certification? This tenth step consists of:

▶ checking the key points of the system implemented last time

▶ if necessary, adjusting the details which might delay certification

▶ preparing the certification audit for each ship.

This last step before the certification process is crucial both for the general management of the company, and the personnel who have invested their time and their efforts to obtain certification. They would find it hard to accept failure. This last inspection is not a luxury, because while error is human, safety and the protection of the environment are values shared by everyone. And human beings have a need for challenges and winning in order to be motivated.

11 Certification

Certification of a system is a binary approach: To be certified or not.

The initial assessment indicates deviations from the requirements of the ISM Code. The final assessment must conclude that the system implemented meets all of the requirements for certification. In other words the recommended approach for the final assessment must indicate a score of 100 per cent for each requirement of the ISM Code after the initial assessment has been carried out.

It is desirable to instruct an external auditor, who has not participated in the implementation of the system, to carry out the final assessment. Objective and neutral, the auditor can quickly detect a weak point or an omission, which might hinder certification. The corrective action undertaken, as a result of this report, will enable those involved to present the certification dossier in complete confidence for:

- shorebased operations

- shipboard

The subject developed in this chapter is based on a logical approach accompanied with practical advice. This is the basis of the project which will enable the company to obtain its certification.

Certification is not an end-goal, but a point of passage for progressing and improving company performance by preventing risks and not by corrective actions which mobilise personnel without any real value. The figure 3.14 shows the safety management cycle which the company should aim to achieve.

In addition to implementing this project, this approach has significant advantages in relation to personnel and costs:

▶ improvement of personnel skills with regard to safety

▶ creation of a company culture motivated around the theme of safety and the environment.

▶ improvement of the kind of conditioned reflex that can prevent a catastrophe or improve the system

▶ reduction of risks of failure, and therefore useless costs.

If these elements can contribute to the overall improvement of the social climate in the company, they can also contribute to better commercial relations. Safety and protection of the environment are essential criteria in keeping with the logic of quality development.

Chapter 5
ISM certification

By resolution A.741 (18) of 4 November 1993, the International Maritime Organisation (IMO) adopted the International Management Code for safety in shipping operations and the prevention of pollution.

In June 1994, the Code became Chapter 9 of the SOLAS Convention. All these decisions imply that any embarkation, covered by the Code's field of application, must be certified on a statutory basis in accordance with the following programme:

■ **July 1996** for passenger ships and ro-ros sailing between ports within the European Union

■ **July 1998** for all passenger ships, oil tankers, chemical tankers, gas tankers and bulk carriers and high-speed cargo ships of at least 500 gt

■ **July 2002** for all other ships and mobile offshore platforms at least 500 gt.

For Europe, certification of passenger ships and ro-ros has been effective since July 1996.

The certification process

The aim of the certification process is to establish that the company is managing safety in accordance with the resolution, based on a very simple principle:

▶ write how activities should be done,

▶ do what has been written,

▶ and be able to prove it.

Certification essentially covers this third point:

▶ checking that a company's safety management system, on shore and on board ship, satisfies the requirements of the ISM Code;

▶ issuing and periodically checking the certificates.

Certification then covers two essential elements in relation to the company and, the ship operations. The on shore operations are the subject of a document of compliance. Ship operations are the subject of a safety management certificate, allocated on an individual basis to each ship, covered previously by the certificate of compliance for the onshore operations of the same company.

Certification can therefore only be given after having demonstrated that the system implemented conforms to the requirements of the ISM Code.

But it is important to hold on to the idea that the purpose of the ISM Code goes beyond certification.

The Code specifies that the company must take all necessary measures to improve its safety system based on the risks that it identifies. It also states that the system implemented must be the subject of periodical checks, by the company and by the flag administration, in order to ensure that the measures taken are maintained in accordance with the fundamental principles of the Code.

The process of certification of safety management consists of three stages:

■ initial certification

■ maintenance of certification

■ re-certification.

Each is the subject of audits on shore and on board ship with a view to issuing, maintaining or renewing the document of compliance and the safety management certificate.

Initial certification

Initial certification only takes place on the first application for certification with a view to issuing a document of compliance to a company, and of a safety management certificate to a ship.

The audits are carried out when the company makes such a request to the administration and/or the classification society authorised by the administration to work towards certification under the ISM Code.

Certification of the system is divided into two phases:

- audit of the shorebased system

- audit of the system on board ship.

While the on-shore audit covers all the marine activities of the company, the audit on board ship is specific to each vessel. Each ship is the subject of an individual audit, even when sister ships are part of the process.

Initial audit of shorebased system

This first assessment is designated under the name initial shorebased audit. The objective is to review and verify the adequacy of the documented systems to see that they cover the requirements of the ISM Code.

At this point, there will be an opportunity for the company to make corrections or adjustments that are indicated by non-conformities raised during the review. These adjustments will have to be made before the audit of the shorebased offices of the company can be processed.

When the documents conform to the requirements of the ISM Code, an audit of the shorebased system is practicable.

The documentary base of the system is essential, because it is not possible to carry out an audit of the system simply based on oral evidence. The code provides the spirit in which the system must be created with a view to meeting company objectives.

When the documentary system conforms to the requirements of the ISM Code, an audit of the shorebased system is required in accordance with a programme. The audit is based on required company procedures, and its purpose is to check that the operational practices actually conform to the written procedures.

When the shorebased audit is complete, the audit team presents its findings at a closing meeting. A written record of the report is given to the company.

If non-conformities are observed, the company must take the necessary measures to ensure that the procedures match the situation observed.

When the audit confirms a match between procedures and the situation observed, a document of compliance can be issued to the company.

Document of compliance

The document of compliance recognises the company's management capacity for safety in the operation of its ships and prevention of pollution. It is issued to the company after the initial shorebased audit fulfils the requirements of the ISM Code.

This initial audit must consider the objective evidence proving that the safety management system has been operating for a minimum of three months, and that it is in force on board each ship operated by the company.

The document of compliance is valid for the types of ship on which the initial shorebased audit was conducted. It can be extended to any other ship after checking that the company is in a position to satisfy the requirements of the ISM Code for the ship type.

Valid for a period of five years, the conformity document is not a certificate, but an essential first stage in the process of certification. A copy of the document should be available on board each ship belonging to the company.

Initial audit of the system on board ship

This second assessment is called the initial shipboard audit. It consists, first, of checking that the documentary systems relating to the ship are available on board and an up to date:

▶ if the documents are available and up to date, the system on board ship is audited as a continuation of the assessment already commenced,

▶ If the documents present deviations compared with the documentary system on shore, the company must take the necessary measures to put the documentary system on board ship into order, before the auditors proceed to the second stage of this audit.

A documentary system is essential in order to carry out an audit of the system on board ship. The auditor cannot interpret the practices based on the ISM Code, so he needs to carry out an audit of the company procedures applicable to the type of ship concerned.

The objectives of the shipboard audit are broadly the same as those for shorebased activities. The emphasis is on the elements of the management systems that are particular to a specific ship type.

The assessment takes a similar form, with interviews of officers and all levels of staff. There is a general inspection of the ship, observation of activities in the workplace, and verification of records.

Among the most important records that are required by the auditors are the class and statutory records of the ship.

If nonconformities are observed during the audit, the company and the master must take the necessary measures to ensure that the procedures match the situation observed.

When the audit confirms that the procedures match the situation a safety management certificate can be issued for the ship.

Safety management certificate

The safety management certificate is the official document which recognises that the safety management and pollution prevention system for each ship is operating effectively. It is issued to a ship at the end of an initial check that the requirements of the ISM Code are being observed.

The initial check must consider the objective evidence which permits certification: the safety management system has been in operation for at least three months on board ship. The objective evidence consists of records specific to the ship, the internal audit file kept by the company as well as the following documents:

▶ the classification certificate certifying that the ship conforms to the requirements of the Resolution A.739 (18) – Ap. 1 – Art. 3 of the IMO;

▶ the statutory certificates required by its supervisory administration;

▶ the statutory inspection and classification files including the observations and comments of the inspectors.

Valid for five years, the safety management certificate is subject, like the company's document of compliance, to intermediate audits.

Maintenance of certification

During the five year period that the document of compliance and the safety management certificate are valid, the system implemented by the company is subject to intermediate audits.

The purpose of these audits is to check, at regular intervals, that the safety management system is operating effectively, and to ensure that any modifications made to the system conform to the requirements of the ISM Code. The frequency of intermediate audits recommended by the IMO is as follows:

■ **Document of compliance:** annually by external audits,

■ **Safety management certificates:** annually by internal audits, and by an external audit between the second and third year after issue of the certificate for the ship.

The flag administration has the authority to decide on the frequency of these audits, in particular during the first years of implementation of the Code.

An intermediate audit must be carried out within a period of three months, before or after each anniversary date of the document of compliance and the safety management certificate by the marine authority. If corrective actions are requested, these must be taken within an agreed period not exceeding three months.

Maintenance of certification therefore covers two aspects:

▶ the shorebased system through the document of compliance,

▶ the ship board system through the safety management certificate.

AUDITS

Shorebased office
Audited every five years
Internal audit every year

Ship
Audited every five years
At least one intermediate verification carried out by external audit
Internal audit annually.

Intermediate audit of the shorebased system

Carried out on the date specified in the programme, this audit consists of: structural and organisational modifications that have a potential impact on the safety management system; the elements of the system which have previously been the subject of non-conformity notices and/or observations; and additional points relating to the safety management system.

The idea is not to repeat the initial audit of the shorebased system, but to ensure that the safety management system includes all of the modifications observed during this period, and that the corrective actions undertaken have borne fruit.

If the company possesses several offices on shore, some of which have not been inspected during the initial audit, an intermediate audit should guarantee that all sites are inspected during the period of validity of the document of compliance.

Examination of modifications made to the documents must include checking that the system still meets the requirements of the ISM Code:

▶ if the modifications made conform to the requirements of the ISM Code, an audit of the shorebased system is then carried out in accordance with the set programme.

▶ if the modifications made do not meet the requirements of the ISM Code, the company must take the necessary measures to remedy this situation, on shore as well as on board ship, within a period of three months.

According to the importance of the modifications observed during the previous appraisal, it is possible that the planned audit may have to be carried out in a similar way to that of an initial audit.

If the review confirms that the documentary system still conforms to the requirements of the ISM Code, the audit of the shorebased system is then undertaken as a continuation of this review.

The audit still relies on company procedures, with the aim of checking that operational practices still conform to the written procedures:

▶ if non-conformities are observed, the company must take the necessary measures to ensure that the procedures match the situation observed,

▶ if the audit confirms that the procedures match the situation observed, the document of compliance is revalidated.

Document of compliance

Maintenance of the document of compliance follows from the external audit carried out by the marine authority for the country in which the company is based, or by an authorised classification society. Validation is carried out annually.

Maintenance of the validity of this document, for on shore operations, is essential, because the loss of validity of this document results in the loss of validity of all safety management certificates issued for the ships managed by the company.

The periodic request for verification for on shore operations must be sent one month before the set date to the administration, or the relevant classification society. Maintenance of the conformity certificate is signified on the initial document.

Intermediate audit of the on board system

Carried out in accordance with the set programme, the system audit on board each ship takes place only after confirmation that the company's document of compliance is to be renewed.

The audit consists of checking that the documents on board ship have been updated, including the elements of the system which have already previously been the subject of non-conformity notices and/or observations, and other additional points relating to the safety management system will be verified.

Once again, the idea is not to repeat the initial audit but to ensure that the safety management system integrates all the modifications observed during this period and that any necessary corrective actions undertaken have born fruit.

The company must undertake to carry out internal audits on board its ships. The results of these are taken into account during the external audit carried out by the administration or a classification society.

Examination of modifications made in the documents on board ship must conclude that the system is still up to date in relation to the audited on shore system.

If the documents are up to date, the system on board ship is audited in accordance with the programme.

If the documents are not up to date, an audit of the system on board ship cannot be carried out. The company must then take the necessary measures to remedy this and set another date for the audit on board ship.

The logic applied for the maintenance of safety management certification on board ship is the same as that relating to the initial audit. The only difference is the extent of the audit, which is more limited.

The external audit consists of checking that the current practices conform to the written procedures specified for the type of ship concerned:

▶ if non-conformities are observed, the company and the master must take necessary action to ensure that measures match the situation observed,

▶ if the audit confirms that measures match the situation observed, the safety management certificate can be revalidated.

Safety management certificate

Maintenance of the safety management certificate for the ship is issued by the marine administration of the country where the ship is registered or by an authorised classification society.

Validating it is carried out between the second and third year of issue. This confirms that the system conforms with the requirements of the Code on board the ship, and that it can be maintained during the period initially allowed.

Maintenance of the certificate is conditional upon maintenance of the document of compliance by the company. The loss of validity of the certificate for a ship does not result in the loss of the document of compliance for the company.

The request for intermediate audits for shipboard operations must reach the administration or classification society one month before the set date.

Re-certification

The entire safety management system for a company is subject to a re-certification process after a period of five years, at the anniversary date of the initial audit. In fact, after five years, the company may well experience major changes in personnel, structure, activities, new acquisitions and so on.

Even if these points were covered during the intermediate audits required for maintenance of certification, a new overall audit of the system is necessary. This covers all the elements of the safety management system, in order to check that all changes and modifications still meet the requirements of the ISM Code.

Re-certification relates to:

■ the shorebased operations for the renewal of the document of compliance.

■ operations on board ship for the renewal of the safety management certificate.

Renewal audit of the company system

The process of re-auditing the company's safety management system is identical to that already described for initial certification.

However, there are two points which should be underlined. During maintenance of certification:

■ the audit relates essentially to the operational implementation of major changes but not necessarily to the detail of the links between the documents.

■ the audits never cover all of the safety management system, but only the points which merit specific attention at a given moment.

The overall re-audit of the company system permits a review of all of the methods implemented including the improvements made.

Renewal of documents

The renewal of the document of compliance and the safety management certificate is the responsibility of the marine administration according to the same provisions as those recommended for the initial certification. By delegation, they can be issued by a recognised classification society.

During this renewal, any modification made to the Code since the initial audit is taken into account in the audit. The assessment of the company's safety system relates to:

- the shorebased operations, for the renewal of the document of compliance,

- the ship board operations for renewal of the safety management system.

Renewal of these two documents must be carried out by the anniversary date of each. It must be planned within a period of six months before the expiry of each document, with the obligation that it is terminated at the date of expiry. If all of the required conditions are satisfied:

▶ a new document of compliance is issued for the company,

▶ a new safety management certificate is issued for the ship.

The period of validity of each is five years. This assumes they are subject to intermediate audits for their maintenance during this new period.

Provisional certificates

If there is a change in flag or company there are provisions to carry out the transition. A provisional document of compliance may be issued to facilitate initial implementation of the ISM Code and its application, when a company has just been created or when an existing document of compliance relates to new types of ships.

A maximum term of 12 months can be granted, having ensured that the company has a safety management system satisfying the requirements of section 1.2.3 of the ISM Code; and that the request is accepted by the marine authority of the country concerned.

A provisional safety management certificate may be issued for a new ship at the time of delivery, and when a company assumes responsibility for it.

A maximum period of six months can be granted after ensuring that the conformity certificate covers the ship concerned by the provisional request.

This last point demonstrates, once again, the importance keeping the document of compliance up to date and in good form.

Safety at sea depends heavily on the interface between the ships at sea and their base on shore.

PART 2
Quality Assurance

Chapter 6
From inspection to ISO 9002

The ISO 9002 Standard, adopted by most industrialised nations of the world today, defines quality assurance.

Quality system registration demonstrates that the client can be confident that the registered company maintains a system that assures best practices in quality, avoids errors, and improves its performance.

ISO 9002 is neither a law nor a set of rules. It is a voluntary way for companies to improve and demonstrate the quality of their management. But more than that: it is now a client requirement.

The evolution of quality

Early in this century, the basic concept of quality was reduced to its simplest expression: the technical performance of a product. Over the course of the last 50 years, its definition has been evolving constantly, not to reflect a greater complexity, but to become closer to the expectations of the client.

The evolution of quality can be explained in relation to a number of different sets of references:

From the 40s to the 60s

This period may be classified as a period of response to growing demands by users of consumer goods. The main concern of companies was to increase their production capacity in order to meet market demand. Availability of the product took priority over other criteria, and consumers did not know their rights, let alone claimed them.

Because many companies made a comfortable profit margin market conditions were not favourable to the development of quality approaches. Nevertheless, work done in North American led certain European manufacturers to introduce more efficient methods of inspecting their products.

A statistical control approach applied to products gradually replaced conventional inspection. Sampling plans by attributes, then by variables, allowed the quality of whole consignments to be estimated on the basis of a representative sample.

These methods, developed before the forties, are still in common use in Europe in many firms, applied to mainly to industrial products.

From the 60s to the 80s

This period may be classified as the time of extensive research into quality control. It was also a period when growing production capacities began to exceed the demands on domestic markets.

Genuine competition existed among manufacturers to reduce production costs. Increasing output without controlling costs became suicidal.

'It is vital to show that an increase in production would be meaningless, until wastage has been stopped. If output is increased, and waste allowed to continue, with nothing done to end it, the new energy produced will only increase this unnecessary waste, and could even lead to unhealthy phenomena'.

Customers were becoming more demanding about product performance, delivery dates and prices. Consumer movements were being set up in many countries to claim their legitimate right to quality products.

In this period market conditions became more favourable to the extension of quality approaches. For a start, statistical techniques applied to products were transferred to manufacturing processes.

This was when most of the statistical methods in use today were introduced on an operational basis. These include control charts, failure trees analysis, value analysis, design analysis and reliability studies.

This was also this period that participatory management, involving quality circles, came to Europe.

From the 80s to the end of the century

This is the time when manufacturers have begun to acknowledged client rights.

Competition is no longer concentrated in existing domestic markets: markets have become globalised, with the survival of every company at stake.

Alliances have been created to improve research, development, production and distribution costs. The aim is to improve overall company performance to meet competition.

Consumer movements have coordinated their forces, and represent a power base that politicians can no longer ignore. They are calling for products that are technically efficient but are safety-oriented, accompanied by good service. Customers remain faithful to a brand only as long as it represents good value.

Quality has become recognised as a strategic factor in corporate policy. Every element in the company has become involved: it is a matter of survival, involving everyone's imagination. It is during this period that participatory management has gained ground, with quality improvement programmes, problem-solving methods, and other quality management schemes.

The concept
Within half a century, the concept of quality has evolved in a remarkable way: from the narrow sense of conformity to a specification, it has opened up to the horizon of appropriate client needs.

This is not to suggest that the first concept was incorrect: rather it has been broadened, and takes account of new consumer expectations, within a socio-economic context that has nothing in common with the previous period.

This change has taken place in successive stages. The evolvement of quality approaches is a reflection of the change in the concept that takes account of these new expectations (figure 6.1, p64).

A new vocabulary has come into existence as the concept has been taken into our working life.

Performance
In considering **performance**, the client expects a product to conform to the technical characteristics announced by the company. This criterion corresponds to the first concept of quality. It remains the fundamental basis, the minimum expected by the client.

Delivery time
Delivery time is brought into the concept of quality when the client may choose, not just performance, but product or service availability. The client may decide to pay for a product or a service that is available when he needs it, and not to wait for one whose performance is similar.

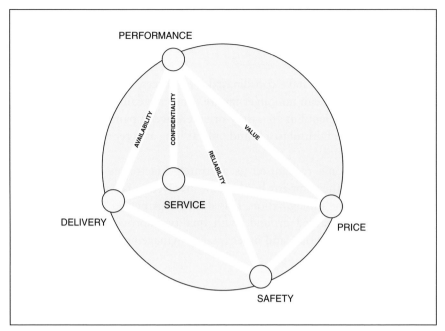

Figure 6.1 The quality pyramid

The relationship between performance and delivery time has led to a new parameter, availability. Companies have had to learn to control this through process flows.

Price

Price entered the quality concept, when society moved from a distribution economy to a market economy.

The client takes account not only of product availability, but also of price, comparing performance offered on the market.

Price used to be related almost solely to the purchasing price. Today, it corresponds to a new parameter factor value. Value is a subjective factor which the client attributes to a product or a service, on the basis of the price he pays and the gratification he gets from its possession - in order words, getting value for money. This is a more important dimension at every economic recession.

The purchasing price criterion also seems to be changing into the concept of 'total cost': the real price paid by the client throughout the useful life of a product until replacement. An example is the real purchasing price of a motor vehicle + insurance premium + maintenance cost + energy costs – resale price.

Service

Recently, under consumer pressure, **service** has entered the concept of quality.

The client understands that he is not buying just a product or a service but paying for 'lifetime' usefulness. An example is the cover offered by a guarantee for household appliances: duration, repair time, temporary loan of similar equipment, and so on.

Service is one of the most important criteria in the evolvement of quality, from the client's point of view.

The relationship between performance and service has given rise to a new parameter, **confidence.** This represents the contractual clauses covering the product and its guarantee. It is a narrow door, and requires a new dialogue between the company and its clients.

In Europe the current trend is create such links between client and companies through quality assurance.

Safety

Formerly included among the technical aspects of performance, *safety,* is now seen as a criterion in its own right.

Now to talk about quality without thinking of safety-consciousness is impossible.

The criterion is taking on an increasingly important dimension in new European standards.

The relationship between expected performance and safety has given fresh importance to the subject of **reliability.** This parameter reflects the arrangements made by the company to protect persons, property and the environment.

New international regulations have been introduced in every sector that sensitive to public opinion. An example for the marine industry is the International ISM Code.

Chapter 7
Understanding ISO 9002

This chapter aims to clarify the ISO 9002 standard as regards the specific activities that need to be read in conjunction with the requirements of the ISM Code.

ISO 9002 is a part of the International Standard for Quality: ISO 9000 series. It is used where a contract between two parties requires demonstration of a supplier's capability to provide the product or service supplied.

Since the last edition of the ISO 9000 series, all standards have 20 requirements with identical clauses for each requirement. The scope of ISO 9002 covers only 18 (below). The two requirements not covered by ISO 9002 are indicated in the text.

ISO 9002 REQUIREMENTS

1. Management responsibility
2. Quality system
3. Contract review
4. Document & data control
5. Purchasing
6. Control of customer supplied product
7. Product identification & traceability
8. Process control
9. Inspection & testing
10. Control of inspection measuring & test equipment
11. Inspection & test status
12. Control of non-conforming product
13. Corrective & preventive action
14. Handling, storage, packaging, preservation & delivery
15. Control of quality records
16. Internal quality audit
17. Training
18. Statistical techniques

These models represent a guide to assist management and executives in introducing a quality and safety management system.

Management responsibility: quality policy

The policy should be a concise and clear statement about the overall intentions and direction of the company about quality, as formally expressed by top management.

It must also define the company commitment to safety and environmental protection.

The purpose is to define quality, safety and environmental protection objectives; and focus and direct the resulting system towards concrete goals.

The company must ensure that this policy is understood, implemented and maintained at all levels in the organisation on ships and in shore based establishments. It must be demonstrated that the policy has the commitment from the chief executive and that all employees understand its content, its objectives, and the commitment displayed by senior management.

Consideration should be given to the policy's interaction with other company policies and procedures. The company should strive to encourage continuous improvement in safety awareness and safety management skills.

The policy should be signed by the chief executive and reviewed at regular intervals to ensure that it remains relevant and effective.

Organisation, responsibility and authority

The responsibility, authority and the interrelation of personnel, both on shore based locations/offices and on ships operations must be defined and documented.

This is to ensure that those involved in the management of quality, safety, and environmental protection know what is expected of them to make the system function effectively.

There should be an organisation chart and defined responsibilities for those activities shown in that chart. Personnel identified should include those who control operations, re-routing, warehousing, delivery, repair etc: and in particular, those who have the authority to take corrective action.

It is necessary to ensure that all ships' personnel comply with the company policy, particularly for those who need the organisational freedom and authority to:

▶ initiate action to prevent non-conformities and to take corrective action

▶ identify and record any quality and safety problems

▶ initiate, recommend or provide solutions through the quality and safety system designed by the company

▶ verify the implementation of solutions.

The level of competence for tasks should be defined. Management should ensure that staff are adequately qualified and fully experienced for the assigned tasks, and that suitable contingency resources have been nominated.

Clear guidance on the master's responsibility and authority on matters affecting the safety of the crew, the environment, the ship and its cargo is an important element in the link between ship and shore. Masters should have adequate authority and be given every encouragement and assistance to implement the system to translate the policy into effective action on board.

The master also has responsibility on board ship for:

▶ implementating company policy

▶ motivating of the crew to observe it

▶ issuing appropriate orders and instructions clearly and simply

▶ verifying that specified requirements are observed, and

▶ revising the quality and safety management system and reporting its deficiencies to the shore based management.

As stated on board a ship, responsibility for quality and safety is primarily the master's, however, it may be delegated to the chief engineer, chief officer, purser, separately or collectively, on a large ship.

Verification, resources and personnel

The company needs to identify these duties and provide adequate resources to perform them. Verification should include both shore and ship inspections, service trials, test and monitoring of the product during storage, transport and delivery of the service.

Quality and safety audits should be carried out by personnel independent of those who are directly responsible for the work being performed. The management representative, or designated person, should be personally responsible for ensuring that audits of the quality and safety system are conducted.

Quality and safety audits can be carried out by a team, but members of the team with direct responsibility for the work should not be in the majority. In very small organisations, a management representative may conduct all audits personally, except for his own responsibilities.

Management representative

As previously discussed, the company should appoint a member of its own management with executive responsibility for quality and safety. He representative may have other jobs, as long as he has adequate freedom when he is acting in his quality and safety capacity.

The designated person should have the responsibility for organising quality and safety audits, and should ensure that corrective action has been taken. This does not override the responsibility of the shipmaster for all actions when the ship is at sea.

The task of implementing and maintaining the quality and safety system is a line-management responsibility. Verification and monitoring activities should be carried out by a person independent of responsibility for implementation.

Management review

The quality and safety system adopted to satisfy the requirements of ISO 9002 and the ISM Code shall be reviewed at appropriate intervals by the company management to ensure its continuing suitability and effectiveness.

Such reviews should recognise the importance of discussions with administrations and organisations representing all relevant interests according to the company scheme for management representative. The frequency of management reviews should be defined.

The agenda for this activity may include review of:

▶ internal quality and safety audits

▶ customer complaints

▶ non-conformities, accidents and hazardous occurrences

▶ sub-contractor performance

▶ training plan

▶ quality and safety improvements

▶ new regulations

▶ market and social trends.

Minutes of management review meetings should be taken and retained. Findings, conclusions and recommendations should be documented. Plans of action to follow up review findings should be documented, and records maintained.

Quality system

According to the requirements of both ISO 9002 and the ISM Code, the system must be documented. (See also Part 1.)

The requirement for a documented system means that a fully comprehensive written description of the company system must be prepared, covering all aspects of the standard and code.

The structure of the documentation is left to each company. It should be borne in mind that each document may be used as the basis for external and internal audits.

The policy of the organisation together with the overall system must be defined. This must be supported by general company procedures, and specific procedures for the ship, which document the activities and associated responsibilities and authority.

Language(s) to be used must be agreed because the procedures are the means of communication on board vessels and between ship and shore personnel.

Where necessary, specific tasks must also be detailed. These documents are termed **work instructions**. A work instruction takes into account variations in operating methods relating to differences in ship design type or ownership.

Government and/or company regulations, quality and safety/training manuals, operational procedures, planned maintenance, quality plan, checklists etc, may be used as part of the documented quality and safety system.

Consideration should also be given to contingency procedures covering emergency situations. A good documented system must cover all the above items and are typically found in:

▶ policy manuals

▶ procedure manuals

▶ operational manuals

according to the size of the company.

Contract review

The company shall establish and maintain procedures for contract reviews and for the co-ordination of these activities. The need to follow this requirement cannot be overemphasised.

Every order accepted from a client should be regarded as a contract and this includes the recording of any verbal communication.

The contract can range from the purchase of a passenger ticket to that for the delivery of valuable goods involving millions of pounds. The agreement between the client and the company must be documented, even when the manager is part of a corporate organisation which is both owner and manager.

The extent to which individual staff can review contracts should be defined and/or reviewed by senior management according to the company procedure.

The conditions of the contract must include, the following where appropriate: However, it is not necessarily limited to these.

▶ limitations on responsibility for operating costs

▶ responsibility for maintenance of the ship

▶ special conditions applicable to the operation of the ship

▶ arrangements for crewing including any requirements above minimum manning levels

▶ reporting arrangements between manager and owner

▶ insurance arrangements and limitations on routes or parts which may be used

▶ lines of communication in case of emergency

▶ restriction on use of agents.

Contract reviews should be recorded. It should be ensured that:

▶ client's requirements are absolutely clear

▶ any differences between the order and the original enquiry and/or the quotation are agreed or resolved

▶ the company is able to meet the terms of the order or contract.

Evidence of review of the agreement, and any changes which may occur during its lifetime, must be documented. Appropriate conditions agreed in the contract should be made available by management to the ship's masters.

Design review
Not required by ISO 9002.

Document, data control, approval and issue
The company should identify what documents and data are needed for safety, quality and pollution prevention. The following gives examples of typical procedures that may be required:

- instructions to master

- ensuring compliance with legislation

- contract review

- purchasing material and equipment

- sub-contractor for servicing crew

- order processing

- order reception

- vessel and product identification and traceability

- vessel modification

- preventive maintenance

- cleaning of tanks and holds

- special operation on board

- emergency

- control of computer systems

- inspection of measuring and testing equipment

- calibration for inspection and measuring equipment

- control of non-conformities

- corrective action

- handling and carriage of hazardous substances

- loading and unloading of products

- storage

▶ auditing and system assessment.

The company will establish and maintain procedures to control all these documents and data. These can be in form of hard copy, electronic or other media.

In addition to internal procedures, plans, data and other documents discussed above, supporting rules, regulations, codes and conventions must be controlled.

A system should be established to ensure that the latest editions and amendments are available at locations where the work is being performed.

Document and data changes modifications

Changes to documents and data need to be reviewed and approved by the organisation that performed the original review and approval, unless otherwise specifically designated. The nature of the change will be identified in the document or the appropriate attachments.

> Be careful!
> It is so simple to make it complicated.

Arrangements must be made to ensure that amendments are notified to the relevant personnel at locations where the work is being performed. Obsolete documents have to be removed, or otherwise assured against unintentional use.

Documents will be re-issued after a practical number of changes have been made (generally after a period of three years).

Purchasing
■ General

Purchasing requirements apply to all those materials, equipment and services in support of the operation that could have an impact on quality, safety and protection prevention. These include sub-contracting of crew, repair, tank cleaning, testing services, training establishments and emergency resources.

■ Evaluation of sub-contractors

Purchasing documents must contain data clearly describing the product or service ordered as mentioned above.

A service provided on the basis of a sub-contract should be under the same control as if the service were provided directly by the company.

The company is responsible for service sub-contracted under the provision of the main agreement, so the company should select sub-contractors on the basis of their ability to meet the requirements. They should seek documented evidence that:

▶ their product or service will meet the specification

▶ that it can do so with consistency and reliability.

It is important that the agreement defines the responsibility for appointmenting agents. The company should decide to what extent supplier (or sub-contractor) approval is necessary, and what should be documented.

Factors which may be taken into consideration include:

▶ vendor appraisal

▶ feasibility

▶ historical evidence

▶ third party certification (such as BVQI).

The company should have a complete list of approved suppliers and sub-contractors, documented with evidence of their performance to comply with the company requirements.

Where regulations required purchased items to be inspected at source by third parties, eg national administrations and classification societies, this requirement should be clearly stated on the purchase order.

■ Purchasing data

Purchasing data must contain data clearly describing the product or service required from the client.

Purchasing documents should be supplied with a clear identification, and applicable issue of specifications, drawings, process requirements, inspection instructions and other relevant technical data; including requirements for approval or qualification of product, service, process equipment and personnel.

Purchasing documents should be reviewed and approved by authorised personnel prior to issue.

■ Verification of purchased product

The company shall be afforded the right to verify at source, or upon receipt, that the purchased product or service conforms to specified requirements.

This requirement relates to the right of the client to impose quality system requirements on the company or sub-contractors.

This right is applicable only where specified in the contracts between the company, the sub-contractor and the client.

■ Purchaser supplied product

It must be clear that, here, the purchaser means the client.

This requirement relates specifically to materials or services provided by the client to be incorporated in, or become part of, the service contracted by the company. For example, in a contract to carry freight or cargo, the company may be required to install a system that enables monitoring of that material.

The company is responsible for recording deviations in quality, safety and quantity from those contracted.

The vessel must be considered as a 'purchaser supplied item' and, where appropriate, so is the crew. Others items which should be considered as purchaser supplied may be trailers, pallets, containers, returnable packaging etc, which may be client-owned property.

Product identification and traceability

When appropriate, the company shall establish and maintain procedures for identifying the client's product while in his care. The degree of identification and traceability may well be the subject of special contractual conditions.

This requirement relates to records which must be controlled so that they can be traced to a particular contract. Equally, goods or passengers must be identifiable to the vessel in which they are being conveyed.

The requirement also relates to the identification of supplies or maintenance components related to specific vessels. So there should be a system for identification of cargo to allow monitoring of maintenance (eg loading lists, bills of loading with mention of any dangerous goods) which must be clearly identified on both loading and, cargo plans, etc.

Process control

The company shall identify and plan activities and events ashore and on board ship to ensure that all operations are carried out, on behalf of the client under controlled conditions to safeguard the quality of the product supplied to him (figure 7.1). These include:

▶ documented procedures and work instructions when needed

▶ monitoring and control of suitable processes and products during storage and handling

▶ approval of processes and equipment as appropriate

▶ criteria for personnel, when appropriate, for special handling.

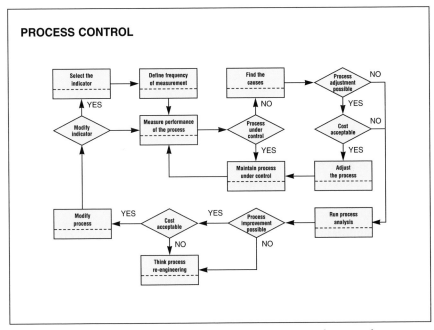

Figure 7.1 Ensure that all operations are carried out under controlled conditions

Procedures and work instructions frequently used may be also classified as follows:

▶ general

▶ the ship in port

▶ preparing for the sea

▶ the ship at sea

▶ preparing for arrival in port.

These are processes where the results cannot be fully verified by subsequent inspection and testing and where, for example, processing deficiencies may become apparent only after an undesirable situation has occurred.

Accordingly, continuous monitoring and/or compliance with documented procedures is required to ensure that the specified requirements are met.

Essential elements of the system, such as stand-by arrangements and the testing of systems which are not continuously active (but are relied upon to work effectively in an emergency) must be considered.

These elements must be classified in two categories:

▶ special operations and

▶ critical operations.

This may be done to prioritise operational planning, and allow the greatest level of attention to be paid to those shipboard operations which are crucial to safety and the protection of the environment.

It is also important that the company shore and shipboard contingency planning is consistent and appropriately integrated.

■ Shore based contingency plans

Shore based contingency plans may include:

▶ the composition and duties of the persons acting within the contingency plan

▶ procedures for the mobilisation of an appropriate company emergency response (which may include the establishment of an emergency response team)

▶ procedures to follow in response to different types of accidents or hazardous occurrences

▶ procedures for establishing and maintaining contact between the ship and management ashore (refer to IMO Assembly Resolution A.648 (16): General Principles for Ship Reporting Systems and Ship Reporting Requirements for further guidance)

▶ the availability of ship particulars, plans, stability information, and safety and environmental protection equipment carried on board

▶ checklists appropriate to the type of emergency which may assist in the systematic questioning of the ship during the response

▶ list of contact names and telecommunication details of all relevant parties who may need to be notified and consulted

▶ reporting methods for both ship and shore based management (refer to IMO A.648 (16))

▶ procedures for notifying and liaising with the next of kin of persons onboard

▶ procedures for issuing information bulletins to and answering queries from the media and the public

▶ back up arrangements for the company's initial response in the event of a protected emergency

▶ the rostering of company personnel and specialists dedicated to support the response and provide adequate relief in the maintenance of routine duties.

■ Shipboard contingency plans

Shipboard contingency plans should take account of the various types of emergency that may arise on a particular ship and may include:

- ▶ the allocation of duties and responsibilities on board

- ▶ actions to be taken to regain control of a situation

- ▶ communication methods to be used on board

- ▶ procedures for requesting assistance from third parties

- ▶ procedures for notifying the company and reporting to relevant authorities

- ▶ maintaining communications between ship and shore

- ▶ procedures for dealing with the media or other outside parties.

Contingency plans should be established to describe how to deal with emergency situations related to damage, fire, pollution, personnel, security and cargo. Examples of emergency preparedness may include:

- ▶ structural failure

- ▶ main engine failure

- ▶ collision

- ▶ explosion

- ▶ grounding

- ▶ cargo spillage.

■ Special shipboard operations

Special shipboard operations are needed when errors become apparent only after hazardous situations have been created or when accidents have occurred.

Procedures and instructions for special shipboard operations should cover precautions and checks that aim to correct unsafe practices and prevent accidents. Examples of special operations include, but are not limited to:

- ▶ ensuring watertight integrity

- navigational safety, including the correction of charts and publications

- operations affecting the reliability of equipment (such as steering gear) and associated standby machinery

- maintenance operations

- bunkering operations and oil transfers in port

- maintaining stability and preventing overloading and overstressing

- lashing of containers, cargo and other items

- ship security, terrorism and piracy.

■ Critical shipboard operations

Critical shipboard operations are those that need to be brought into effect when an error may cause an accident, immediately or a situation which could threaten life, the environment or the ship.

Particular attention should be drawn to the need to adhere to strict instructions in the conduct of critical operations, and satisfactory performance should be closely monitored. Examples of critical operations include:

- navigation in confined waters or high density traffic areas

- operations that may cause a sudden loss of manoeuvrability in close or high density traffic waters

- navigation in conditions of reduced visibility

- operations in heavy weather conditions

- the handling and stowage of hazardous cargoes and noxious substances

- bunkering and oil transfer at sea

- cargo operations on gas, chemical and oil tankers and

- critical machinery operations.

Arrangements should be put in place to monitor the operational competence of crew undertaking critical shipboard operations.

■ Emergency preparedness

The company should establish procedures to identify, describe and respond to potential emergency situations on board ship (figure 7.2).

The company should also establish programmes for drills and exercises to prepare for emergency actions.

The safety management system should provide measures to ensure that the company's organisation can respond at any time to hazards, accidents and emergency situations involving its ships:

▶ steering gear failure

▶ electrical power failure

▶ collision

▶ grounding/stranding

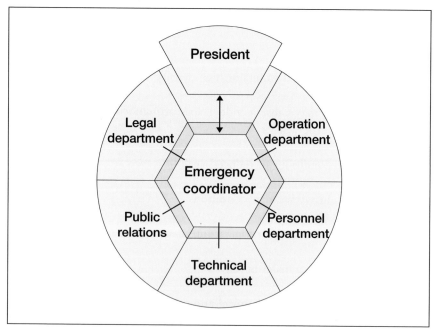

Figure 7.2 Emergency prepardness organisation

- ▶ shifting of cargo

- ▶ cargo spillages or contamination

- ▶ fire

- ▶ cargo jettisoning

- ▶ flooding

- ▶ machinery room casualty

- ▶ abandoning ship

- ▶ man overboard/search and rescue

- ▶ entry into enclosed spaces

- ▶ serious injury

- ▶ terrorism or piracy

- ▶ helicopter operations and

- ▶ heavy weather damage.

The list is by no means exhaustive and the company should attempt to identify all possible situations where shipboard contingency planning is be required, relative to the ship, its construction, equipment and trade.

■ Emergency drills

Actions to counter potential emergencies should be practised in drills. A programme of such drills, additional to those required by the SOLAS Convention, should be carried out regularly to develop and maintain the confidence and proficiency of the personnel who may be involved in actual emergencies.

Rudin's Law

In crises that force people to choose between alternative courses of action, most people will choose the worst possible one.

These drills should be developed to exercise the emergency plans established for critical situations and should, as appropriate, mobilise the shore based management emergency contingency plans under simulated conditions.

Records of all emergency drills and exercises conducted ashore or on board, should be maintained and made available for verification purposes.

Appropriate personnel should evaluate the results of these drills and exercises as an aid to determining the effectiveness of documented procedures.

Inspection and testing
■ Receiving inspection and testing

The company shall ensure that incoming material is not used until it has been inspected or otherwise verified as conforming to specified requirements.

Receiving inspection should include the inspection or verification of new equipment and spares, as well as reconditioned or second hand material or equipment, used in the operation of the vessel or the service.

It should also include any receiving inspection of the client's cargo/freight, whether specified in the contract or not. This may be carried out by the company or an agent appointed by the client.

■ In-process inspection

The company shall inspect product and material as required by the procedures and identify non-conforming product and material.

These operations may be performed on board or ashore to ensure the safe and satisfactory execution of the service.

Procedures should define the need for, and the frequency of, any in-process inspections carried out. Results of any such inspections should be formally recorded.

The inspection or monitoring of the service should include a check for damage, contamination of cargo etc.

In-process inspection should include the inspection of vessels and facilities in use, ie after cleaning or maintenance. It could also include any sampling or tests of the cargo in store or transit as specified in the contract: for example, monitoring of temperature.

The inspection should be a continual process.

■ Final inspection and testing

The company shall carry out all final inspections and testing in accordance with the requirements of the contract. No product shall be released until all the activities specified by the procedures have been completed and documented satisfactorily.

Final inspection and testing should include any inspection and testing specified in the contract prior to release from storage or a point of delivery.

Final inspection or monitoring of the service could also include checks in late delivery, damage, contamination, and customer surveys where relevant.

■ Inspection and test records

The company shall establish and maintain records which provide evidence that the product or service has passed inspection with defined acceptance criteria.

The company should state in a documented system what records (eg log books) are kept, for how long and by whom. Records may include:

▶ equipment maintenance and modification records

▶ fleet operations performance records

▶ lashing gear and/or twist locks

▶ tank storage and cleaning listing.

Control of inspection, measuring and test equipment

The company shall control, calibrate and maintain inspection, measuring and test equipment to demonstrate that the product or service conforms to the specified requirements.

Measurements required to establish that the service is being provided in accordance with the contract should be undertaken using measuring equipment of known accuracy. This is to be achieved by regular calibration, in accordance with the requirements of the standard for each specific type of equipment.

The types of equipment which should be covered include:

▶ pressure gauges

▶ temperature gauges

▶ equipment associated with maintenance, including torque tools, gauges or cleaning equipment.

The following guidance relates to this chapter, as indicated:

▶ the accuracy required is for the most stringent measurements for which that equipment is used

▶ no matter how many comparisons are made during the calibration process, the records should ensure that it is possible to trace back to national standards

▶ instrumentation associated with the measurement of quality, in terms of the product transported, the transportation service, and maintenance and repair of the vessels should be identified, marked and controlled according to these requirements.

▶ if gauges are available for maintaining product quality or quantity, these should be either calibrated or labelled to indicate that they are or not calibrated.

In addition to measuring equipment used for length, volume, temperature, pressure or weight measurements, the requirement also applies to navigation equipment, software, loading instruments and measurements used in the operation of on board equipment and in cargo monitoring.

Where the measurements are sub-contracted to an inspection agent, the company remains responsible for ensuring that equipment used by the agent is calibrated.

Inspection and test status

The inspection and test status shall be identified by using markings, authorised stamps, tags, labels and inspection records which indicate the conformance or non-conformance of the product or material with regard to inspection and tests performed.

Records must identify the inspection authority responsible for the release of non-conforming items.

Means of identifying the status of inspections and checks at each stage of the service need to be provided. These must include the status of the crew, the vessel, its equipment, cargo and its progress in relation to planned events and in emergencies.

For equipment it should include, for example:

▶ pressure test on tanks

▶ inspection of tanks after cleaning

▶ test on pressure release valves, lashing gear etc.

The clause also applies to any inspections or tests on the client's product which may be called up in the contract. It is also relevant during repair and maintenance of vessels and equipment; for example the suitability of parts removed for re-use and inspection of tanks after cleaning.

Control of non-conforming product or service

The company shall establish and maintain procedures to ensure that product or material that does not conform to specified requirements is prevented from inadvertent use or installation.

In general for the industry, the non-conforming product comprises equipment used in the service which is defective or out of service for some other reason.

Procedures are required for dealing with non-conformities which directly affect the client or the safety on board.

Non-conformities may result from various incidents, and systems need to be established for dealing with them. Consideration should be given to:

▶ equipment and personnel failures

▶ complaints internal and external

▶ accident reporting

- force-majeure contingencies

- contaminated or damaged loads

- incorrect quantities of a load

- badly packed or badly loaded clients' products

- subcontractor performance not complying to specifications.

The service itself should be reviewed to identify consignments running early or late, to wrong destination or collection point, unsuitable equipment accident reporting etc. The responsibility and authority for dealing with all forms of incidents should be defined.

Corrective and preventive action

The company shall establish, document and maintain procedures for investigating the cause of non-conforming products and service, and the corrective action needed to prevent and recurrence (figures 7.3, 7.4).

The aim of this requirement is to eliminate the root causes of non-conformity by initiating preventative action, and then ensuring that corrective and preventive actions taken are effective.

Corrective and preventive action procedures should be implemented in the event of:

- any failure of the quality and safety system

- complaints from customers

- complaints to company or sub-contractor.

The quality and safety system should require the master to report the following to the designated person(s) ashore:

- accidents

- hazardous occurrences

- non-conformities within the SMS and

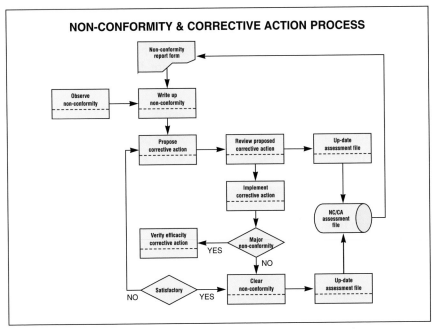

Figure 7.3 *Non-conformity must be investigated*

NON-CONFORMITY: SHIP REPORT

Ship name: [   ]   Report No: [   ]

☐ Major non-conformity

☐ Non-conformity

Description of the non-conformity:

Date: _____   Auth. person

☐ Pending ◯

☐ Non-confirmity cleared

Corrective action:

Date: _____   Master

Date: _____

Designated person

Corrective action follow-up:

Date: _____   Auth. person   Master

Figure 7.4 *Corrective action must be documented*

▶ suggested modifications and improvements to the SMS.

When these reports are received by the designated person ashore they should be reviewed and evaluated by the appropriate level of management to determine corrective action to ensure that recurrences are avoided.

Accidents and hazardous occurrences should always be reported (figures 7.3, 7.4). Reports should include a description of the probable causes; details of the consequences with respect to harm to people; damage to the environment, of property, or the loss of operational safety; and any suggestions for improvement.

Any deviation from the SMS procedures and instructions (a non-conformity) should be documented and, in accordance with procedures established in the SMS, reported as required to shore-based management.

The SMS should be designed to allow for continual updating, amendment and improvement resulting from the analysis of accidents, hazardous occurrences and non-conformities, and changed circumstances within the company.

The company should have a system for recording, investigating, evaluating, reviewing and analysing reports, and for taking action as appropriate.

Necessary feedback through the master should be provided to those persons who have raised concerns through the appropriate procedures.

Feedback is an important motivator and should assist in encouraging further effective reporting. Feedback should include an acknowledgement the receipt of the report, its status and any final decisions made.

The evaluation of reports may result in:

▶ corrective and preventive action being taken

▶ distribution of experiences throughout the company

▶ amendment to existing SMS procedures and instructions, or

▶ the development of new SMS procedures.

Handling, storage and packaging
■ General
The company shall establish and maintain procedures for the handling, storage, packaging and delivery of products.

The requirement applies, as appropriate, to any material supplied by the client and also to items used in repair and maintenance, including the vessel itself and passengers.

When developing procedures for handling, storage, packaging and delivery, due consideration must be given to potential safety and pollution hazards.

■ Handling
The company shall provide methods of handling that prevent damage or deterioration.

The requirement relates to the provision of safe and secure handling procedures, including the prevention of contamination. If not already covered by process control, handling procedures should address, for example, loading and unloading, and special handling for hazardous products.

■ Storage
The company shall provide secure areas or stock rooms to prevent damage or deterioration of product and material, pending use or delivery.

This requirement is particularly important both on shore and on the vessel, where storage is under the company's direct control. If not already covered by process control, procedures should address all storage aspects including:

▶ purchaser's products

▶ spare parts used in the maintenance of the service

▶ any other item in store.

Topics that may need to be addressed include:

▶ stock rotation

▶ special storage conditions such as temperature

- storage of hazardous products

- segregation of non-compatible items

- stacking heights

- securing arrangements

- partially filled tanks (eg effect on stability).

■ Packaging

The company shall control packing, packaging, preservation and marking processes to the extent necessary to ensure conformance to specified requirements; and shall identify, preserve and segregate all products from the time of receipt until the company's responsibility ceases.

Procedures should address packing and packaging techniques: for example those that may be suitable for land transportation but would not survive a normal sea voyage.

Control of quality records

The company shall establish and maintain procedures for identification, collection, indexing, filing, storage, maintenance and disposition of quality and safety records.

Records can be in the form of hard copy, or they may be in electronic or other media. A record control system should be defined that ensures documents are stored in an orderly and retrievable manner.

Some records may remain in the vessel, others may require to be transferred to storage on shore. The record system must comply with any statutory, national or international requirements for record retention.

Retention periods for quality records should be defined. Quality and safety records required by the standard include:

- approved sub-contractors

- calibration

- contract review

▶ corrective action

▶ inspection and tests

▶ internal audits

▶ management review

▶ non-conforming product

▶ purchase orders

▶ training.

Procedures should define where records are held, how they are filed, who is responsible for records, and how the records are disposed.

Internal quality audits

The company shall carry out internal audits to verify whether quality, safety and pollution prevention activities comply with planned arrangements, and to determine the effectiveness of the company system.

Consequently it is necessary periodically to audit each element of the system, covering all activities carried out both on board and ashore according to a pre-planned schedule of internal audits.

Audit plans should be established and should encompass all departments involved with the quality and safety system and each individual's ship. Relevant sections of the company should be audited over a reasonable period of time. The plans should cover:

▶ the specific areas and activities to be audited

▶ the qualifications of personnel carrying out the audits, and

▶ procedures for reporting findings, conclusions and recommendations.

Senior management should receive regular reports on the continuity, suitability and effectiveness of the quality and safety system. These reports should be presented by personnel responsible for the conduct of this system.

Objective evaluations of results from audits should be conducted by competent personnel and should review:

▶ organisational management structures

▶ administrative procedures

▶ personnel, including their responsibilities and authority

▶ familiarity with, and adherence to, the quality, safety and environment protection policies procedures and instructions

▶ requirements for additional familiarisation or 'on the job' training, and

▶ documentation reports and record keeping.

Corrective actions should be checked by the auditor after implementation.

Training

The company shall establish and maintain procedures for identifying the training needs, and provide the training of all personnel activities affecting quality, safety and pollution prevention.

The training system adopted should generate objective evidence that individual staff have met the training requirements. On the job training may frequently be appropriate in meeting this requirement.

Part of the identification of training needs relates to the company's recruitment policy, which should be stated, as well as the policy of training for crew familiarisation of the vessel.

The company should ensure that masters are properly qualified for command, and fully conversant with the company quality and safety management system.

All personnel, both on board and ashore, must be trained in all aspects of the management system relevant to the work they are required to undertake.

Managerial personnel who have a decision making responsibility, or who are responsible for directing other personnel, should be trained in managerial techniques necessary to carry out their duties effectively.

New personnel, and personnel transferred to new assignments, must receive proper familiarisation with their duties, and have an adequate understanding of relevant rules, regulations, codes and guidelines.

Safety training drills should be carried out in accordance with the procedures and requirements laid down in the SMS.

The drills should cover likely emergency situations and should aim to ensure that crew members meet the company's safety management standard, and gain confidence in controlling situations that are likely to arise should an emergency occur.

Results of safety audits, drills and the analysis of accidents, hazardous occurrences and non-conformities may assist in identifying additional company training requirements or necessary changes to safety procedures.

The company should consider ways of reviewing individual training needs and for, check the validity of recorded qualifications, in line with international, national and special company requirements.

The company should consider the establishment of procedures for the conduct of refresher courses for personnel engaged in critical safety and emergency operations safety.

Servicing

Not required by ISO 9002.

Statistical techniques

In cases where inspections are conducted by a sample process, the technique adopted should be statistically valid.

The selected sample size and methodology should, where appropriate, comply with recognised published techniques.

The company shall establish and maintain procedures for implementing and control the application of statistical techniques as needed.

Chapter 8
How to implement ISO 9002

The approach adopted in this chapter is similar to that already used for implementing the ISM Code. This approach offers a company considerable flexibility in choosing which reference document to apply, and in arranging the scheduling of operations.

▶ The reference document may be confined to ISO 9002, for the certification of a quality system. It could also comprise both ISO 9002 and the ISM Code, in order to obtain dual certification, covering not only the quality system but also safety management of ship operation and environmental protection.

▶ Since the approach for implementation of both reference documents is much the same, they may be applied simultaneously or separately. When application involves two separate stages, the workforce does not need to be retrained, since it has already acquired the basic skills. Only training in the second reference document is necessary. Because of these similarities, I recommend cross-checking the two methodologies step by step.

The 10 steps in this programme are:

1   Initial audit

2   Strategic planning

3   Quality policy

4   Responsibilities and authority

5   Quality team

6   Quality manual

7   Quality procedures

HOW TO IMPLEMENT ISO STANDARD	4.1 Management responsibility	4.2 Quality system	4.3 Contract review	4.5 Document control	4.6 Purchasing	4.7 Purchaser supply product	4.8 Product ident & traceability	4.9 Process control	4.10 Inspection & testing	4.11 Insp measure & test equip.	4.12 Inspection & test status	4.13 Control non conf. product	4.14 Correct & prevent action	4.15 Hand. stor. pack. & delivery	4.16 Quality records	4.17 Internal quality audits	4.18 Training	4.20 Statistical techniques
Initial audit	1																	
Strategic planning	2																	
Quality policy	3																	
Responsibilities & authority	4																	
Quality team	5																	
Quality Manual		6	7	8	9	10	11	12	13	14	15	16	17	18	19			
Quality Procedures						10	11	12	13	14	15	16	17	18	19			
Measurement & reporting																		20
Personnel training																	21	
Prequalification audit	21																	

Figure 8.1 Schedule for implementation of the ISO 9002 Standard

8 Measurement and reporting

9 Training

10 Pre-qualification audit.

Figure 8.1 presents the general schedule for implementation of ISO 9002.

1 Initial audit

Objective: identify actions that need to be taken, ashore and aboard, to bring the quality system into line with ISO 9002.

This first step involves:

▶ assessing current company practice against the requirements of ISO 9002

▶ identifying deviations from the 18 relevant sections of ISO 9002

▶ supplying company management with information on any discrepancies, and on sectors where improvements would be needed to obtain ISO 9002 certification.

The initial assessment covers all company operations ashore and on board its ships. It starts with an analysis of company quality policy, and how company requirements are taken into account in the documentary system.

Not all ships are surveyed during this assessment, but at least one vessel used for each type of activity needs to be inspected, in order to reveal any deviations from ISO 9002 requirements.

If dual certification is being sought by the company, both reference documents are, of course, applied at this stage.

The results of the initial assessment provide a reference against which to measure progress as the project advances.

The initial review of the system can be carried out according to the model format shown on page xx.

2 Strategic planning

Objective: achieve implementation of ISO 9002 ashore and aboard, in due time and at reasonable cost.

This second step involves:

▶ establishing the timetable for actions to be taken, sequence by sequence, on shore and aboard ship

▶ defining and adopting realistic deadlines for each action

▶ identifying the resources and means needed to achieve the project by the agreed deadline.

Following the report obtained by the initial audit, it is necessary to take the time to plan the action to be undertaken in the time given. Implementation of the action plan may take between 16 and 24 months before the company is ready for certification.

Not all the points below have to be taken into consideration, but the fact of asking these questions may avoid forgetting something important.

Initial audit of the system

operational planning at head office, on shore and shipboard
documentary review of the existing system at head office
audit of the shore-based system
audit of the system on board the ships selected
preparation of the audit report
presentation of the report to the company management.

Strategic planning

management seminar on ISO 9002
definition of priorities, trends and objectives
preparation of the action plan
approval of the action plan.

Quality policy

development of the policy draft
final review of the policy
commitment of general management
formalisation of the policy
internal/external communication plan
presentation to personnel
implementation.

Responsibilities and authority

company flowcharts
definition of responsibilities, authority and operational links
head office and on shore-based centres
management representative
master and officers on board ship.

Quality team

definition of the task
selection of members
definition of responsibilities, authority and operational links
training in project and team work
providing information to personnel

launching of the project.

Quality manual

development of the documentary structure
planning of the preparation of a documented system
drafting of the company manual
approval of the company manual
publishing the company manual.

Quality Procedures

detailed review of existing procedures
identification of documentary requirements
planning the preparation of the procedures
drafting the procedures
approval of the procedures
publishing the procedures
implementing of the procedures.

Measurement and reporting

content, form and frequency of the report
responsibility for preparation
role of general management.

Personnel training

identification of requirements
preparation of the training programme
approval of the training programme
training of management
personnel and internal auditors
appraisal of training courses.

Pre-qualification audit

planning the audits
designation of the auditor
realisation of the audits
presentation of the report to the general management of the company

implementation of corrective actions, if necessary

preparation of the certification request file.

This initial strategic planning will probably be reviewed after several months to make it more realistic. The advantage is that, having prepared it, and knowing what is being modified and why, determines the expected result.

At this crucial stage of the programme, a single strategic plan is sufficient, if the company is aiming for dual certification. If the company's own resources are inadequate, it should call upon external assistance. It would be quite unrealistic to imagine that the programme can be implemented during normal business.

3 Quality policy

Objective: assert company policy by displaying management's commitment to the programme.

This third step involves:

▶ drafting company quality policy

QUALITY & SAFETY POLICY

The success of our mission depends primarily on the combined skills available in our organisation. It is our policy to ensure that every employee works under conditions of safety. In the face of international competition, we need more than ever to be attentive to and satisfy the needs of every single client. A satisfied client is a loyal client. It is our policy to deliver service to every client, in accordance with the terms of signed contracts, by stated deadlines, and at the lowest cost. This action, which is vital for the future, is conceivable today only if we also assume our responsibilities within the indispensable international environment.

It is our policy to provide, according to plan, all the provisions needed to ensure and maintain safety on every one of our ships, and maintain safety on every one of our ships, and to prevent any risk of pollution. To comply with all these commitments, we also need to earn the necessary profits, to keep ourselves at the very highest level in these areas, for the satisfaction of our clients and ourselves. It is out policy to implement a permanent quality and safety improvement programme, with the participation of the whole workforce. In my capacity as Chairman of Axe Maritime Co. Ltd., I make my personal commitment to this policy, and rely on your participation.

Figure 8.2 A global policy

▶ informing all the personnel of the importance of the programme for the company's future, its contents and the planned schedule for its introduction

▶ emphasising management expectations of the personnel while still displaying the commitment of every member of management.

If quality policy is being drawn up with the aim of dual certification, this is bound to strengthen the links that exist between quality and safety. The company should have a single policy to cover both subjects, since there is common goal.

Figure 8.2 is an example of quality policy linked to the safety and environmental protection policy presented in Part 1 of this book.

4 Responsibilities and authority

Objective: ensure that the programme covers all activities needed to maintain the intended level of quality.

Once quality policy is established, the role of every protagonist needs to be defined, in implementing and maintaining the policy.

MASTER
RESPONSIBILITIES & AUTHORITY

–Implement Quality, Safety & EP policy
–Ensure that policy is clearly displayed and promoted.
–Ensure that policy is understood by all crew members
–Issue orders & instructions in clear manner
–Familiarize crew members
–Verify Q&SMS application on board
–Review Q&SMS on board
–Conduct drills & exercises
–Prepare & issue watchkeeping role
–Designate deck officer duty officers
–Report deficiencies to shorebased management
–Make immediate decisions in the best interests of the safety of the
  crew, ship & environment.

Figure 8.3 Clear responsibilities and authority

This fourth step involves:

▶ defining responsibilities and authority at every level of organisation (figure 8.3)

▶ establishing the clearest and simplest functional links among the various departments, ashore and on board company vessels

▶ issuing documents on the responsibilities and authority of different departments, and functional links among them.

These documents form part of the company quality manual, and must be available at all times on-shore and on board ships.

Together with quality policy, the documents provide the starting point for any certification audit, prior to obtaining or maintaining such certification.

5 Quality team

Objective: develop and carry out the actions needed to obtain certification of the company quality system, and solve any problems that could have an adverse effect on the expected result.

Success depends on the commitment and participation of every member of management. However, it is important for the company to entrust the task to a special team.

The fifth step involves:

▶ appointing members of the project team

▶ designating a project manager, to coordinate all actions needed to achieve the intended goal

▶ assigning responsibilities within the project team

▶ undertaking actions to schedule and in accordance with the responsibilities assigned to each team member.

Each step of the management loop must be developed as for the implementation of the ISM Code:

- ▶ establish correct document

- ▶ perform according to document

- ▶ audit the activities

- ▶ review the system prior certification.

The project manager should be accountable directly to the managing director. Team members coordinate all the actions needed, each within his particular area. Each head of department is responsible for implementing actions within his department.

Again, there are clear advantages in dual certification, since it is the same team that coordinates all actions, within a single project.

6 Quality manual

Objective: set out the rules for applying company quality policy, in order to inspire confidence in its clients and to provide proof of quality.

The quality manual comprises a statement of quality policy; the organisation chart, with job description showing responsibilities and authority, means and resources deployed; and a description of the quality system, showing the measures introduced to comply with the requirements of ISO 9002.

This sixth step involves:

- ▶ setting up the documentary structure needed to produce the quality manual

- ▶ writing documents specifying the quality system, in accordance with ISO 9002

- ▶ establishing the rules for maintenance and further development of the quality system.

The quality manual should be available in all units, ashore and aboard.

This general document should also be available to all clients, whenever a contract is being negotiated or renewed. Amendments must be indicated clearly.

The quality manual needs to be revised periodically to ensure that it remains relevant, and must be adapted to meet requirements and new company policies.

7 Quality procedures

Objective: describe clearly and as simply as possible all the specific actions needed to maintain company quality policy.

Procedures are an integral part of the company documentary system. They must cover activities both on-shore and aboard ship, as well as interfaces between onshore units and ships.

The first action to be taken usually involve onshore centres, to make it possible to control the system set up to meet ISO 9002 requirements. As the documentary system is completed on shore, attention must be paid to ships and the interfaces needed to make the system operational.

This seventh step involves:

▶ cataloguing procedures already existing among company documents

▶ analysing each existing procedure in terms of conformity to ISO 9002

▶ identifying deficiencies in the system

▶ writing or rewriting missing or obsolete procedures

▶ constructing the company documentary system in conformity to ISO 9002.

Responsibility for writing the procedures should be held by each head of department, with all necessary participation by shipmasters.

The architecture of the documentary system should be designed to form two specific manuals:

▶ onshore procedures

▶ shipboard procedures.

Wherever necessary, procedures may be accompanied by instructions. All these documents require periodic revision, to keep them relevant and control changes. Amendments must be indicated clearly.

Finally, procedures should be available on-shore and aboard ship, in accordance with the documentary system architecture.

8 Measurement and reporting

Objective: allow management to oversee the state of progress of the project, and intervene when required.

The period needed for complete implementation of the quality system depends on numerous criteria such as size of the company, nature and number of ships, internal resources. Many months may elapse before the goal is reached.

Involved as they are in day-to-day operations, those involved in the project may postpone actions because of lack of time or emergencies and deadlines can be missed.

This eighth step involves:

▶ right at the start, drawing up a timetable of meetings to examine the state of progress of the project

▶ setting up a project monitoring system under the direct responsibility of the project manager

▶ identifying discrepancies and their causes

▶ taking necessary corrective action to respect deadlines or, in the last resort, alter the timetable for actions.

The presence and direct involvement of company management is vital at such meetings. Management thereby confirms its determination to see the project through, and helps motivate the team responsible for carrying it out.

9 Personnel training

Objective: develop and improve the abilities of shore based and on board personnel, in terms of company quality policy.

However all-embracing and sophisticated the documentary system may be, it will not in any practical result unless the workforce has access to information that it can understand.

This ninth step involves:

▶ preparing a training cycle for all those with responsibility for implementing the new system

▶ making arrangements to ensure that knowledge of the system introduced onshore and aboard ship is properly relayed

▶ arranging for training new recruits, to keep the system operational

▶ arranging the necessary training, when changes are made in the system

▶ training the personnel in accordance with the training cycle

▶ training internal assessors to ensure that the quality system is maintained properly.

The best training manual for executives and other personnel is a well-drafted account of procedures.

Specific technical subjects can be learnt through videocassettes. Imagination is needed to maintain the capability of the workforce.

10 Pre-qualification audit

Objective: demonstrate that the quality system introduced within the company will meet requirements for ISO 9002 certification.

This step represents the culmination of the whole project, to obtain official certification of the company quality system.

Several months will have elapsed between the initial assessment and the pre-qualification assessment, with many ups and downs. Is the company finally ready for certification?

This tenth step involves:

▶ making a final check on key points in the new system

▶ if necessary, correcting any details that might delay certification

▶ preparing the application file for certification of the whole company.

This final step, prior to the certification process, is crucial not just for company management, but also for the individuals who have invested time and effort in obtaining certification. Failure would be hard for them to accept.

The initial audit indicated any deviations from the requirements of ISO 9002. The pre-qualification audit must conclude that the system implemented meets all the requirements for certification. In other words, the recommended approach for the final assessment must indicate a score of 100 per cent for each requirement of the standard after the initial audit has been carried out.

It is desirable to instruct an external auditor, who has not participated in the implementation of the system, to carry out the pre-qualification audit. Objective and neutral, the auditor can quickly detect a weakness or an omission which might hinder certification. The corrective action undertaken, as a result of this report, will enable those involved to present the certification dossier in complete confidence for:

▶ shore-based operations

▶ shipboard.

The subject developed in this chapter is based on a logical approach, accompanied with practical advice. This approach will help enable the company to obtain its certification.

The main reason presenting the implementation of ISO 9002 standard in the same way as the implementation of the ISM Code is to convince you that quality system and safety systems are linked together. These links will be developed in the next chapter.

Chapter 9
Certification scheme for integrated systems

Under increasing pressure from authorities and clients, maritime transportation companies are being forced to provide proof of the quality of their management and organisation.

Possession of a uniform set of statutory certificates, usually referring to technical regulations and codes, is no longer sufficient to demonstrate a company's good management techniques.

Companies have to comply with new mandatory international requirements, culminating in certification of provisions for safety on board ships, and prevention of pollution risks.

They also have to meet the requirements of their clients, and prove that personnel on board each ship possess the skills needed to ensure that all the tasks involved in proper functioning of the ship are performed properly.

The administrative arrangements needed to handle all these new requirements may seem complicated, expensive and difficult to implement, or even appear to conflict with profit-earning considerations.

The same question is raised at many seminars: 'Can ISO 9002 be regarded as equivalent to ISM Certification?', 'Is there any connection between ISO 9002 and the ISM Code?'.

This chapter presents the key items in each of the new reference standards, in order to identify the points they have in common. It also offers a new view of certification, helping to simplify the system.

Present systems
The two main references to be taken into account are the ISM and ISO 9002.

However, in addition to these codes, there are the mandatory requirements of the new Convention on Standard of Training, Certification and Watchkeeping for Seafarers (STCW).

Because of their individual areas of application, management of each of these three reference documents involves different aspects. They may overlap, but should never duplicate one another.

ISM Code

The ISM Code is the culmination of a long period of discussion about the need to reach some solution to improve safety at sea and prevent the risk of pollution.

Since May 1994, it has formed the new chapter 9 of the international Convention on the Safety of Human Life at Sea (SOLAS). The fundamental principle of the ISM Code is that improvement in safety at sea depends on changes in behaviour, and that human effort is the key to success.

The ISM Code contains 13 chapters:

Safety and environmental protection management system

Safety and environmental protection policy

Company responsibilities and authority

Designated person(s)

Master's responsibility and authority

Resources and personnel

Development of plans for shipboard operations

Emergency preparedness

Reports and analysis of non-conformities, accidents and hazardous occurrences

Maintenance of the ship and equipment

Documentation

Company verification, review and evaluation

Certification, verification and control.

All the provisions to be introduced by the company go to form the safety management and pollution prevention system. This system is periodically assessed, and subject to renewal after five years.

The ISM Code focuses on four aspects:

Management commitment and responsibility

Personnel competence and involvement

Good condition of equipment and maintenance

Inspection and risk-prevention methods.

The regulatory nature of the Code makes it mandatory for companies in the maritime transport sector. The Code comes into effect according to a timetable (see p48).

ISO 9002 requirements

The ISO 9002 standard, adopted by the International Organisation for Standardisation, concerns quality management within the framework of contractual relations between a company and its clients.

Its origins date from 1987, when companies, seeking a way of reducing the number of audits they were forced to face by their industrial clients, under audits from suppliers

ISO 9002 was revised in 1994, to adapt it to other sectors of business. It is now used world-wide to certify quality systems. The basic intention of this standard is to provide a client with adequate assurance that the expected service will meet his requirements.

ISO 9002 contains 18 paragraphs: (see p 66).

All these provisions, implemented by the company, form the quality management system.

ISO 9002 focuses mainly on four points:

▶ Management commitment and responsibility

▶ Contract review

▶ Production process control

▶ Methods of inspection and prevention of quality deficiencies.

The status of such standards means that ISO 9002 is neither a legal obligation, nor a set of rigid rules. Rather, it offers a way of achieving voluntary improvement in the quality of a company's services, and of demonstrating it. However, with the passage of time, and as experience increases, clients are increasingly demanding its implementation.

STCW Convention

The STCW Convention, adopted by IMO in 1978, defines standards for training, certification and watchkeeping for seafarers.

This Convention, which was revised in 1995, reinforces the criteria for eligibility of seafarers, and requires proof of the effectiveness of measures introduced to satisfy the intentions of the Convention.

We have covered the minimum compulsory standards for the qualification and certification of the skills of seafarers, namely, apart from general provisions for implementation of the Convention:

▶ requirements for master and seafarer

▶ requirements for engine room crew

▶ requirements for radio operators

▶ specific requirements concerning certain types of ships

▶ requirements concerning safety, emergencies, medical care and conditions of survival at sea

▶ conditions for maintaining certification of seafarers during the transitional period provided for in the Convention

▶ requirements to be respected for surveillance at sea in order to ensure the safety of those on board during a voyage.

The regulatory nature of the STCW Convention means that there is no way that maritime transport companies can avoid it. All these provisions concern maritime administration, training bodies and companies.

Every company must be able to prove that seafarers on board its ships possess the skills needed to perform the functions assigned to them. They also have to set up a further training programme, to maintain and even develop such skills.

The STCW Convention is to be implemented internationally according to a timetable:

■ On **1 February 1997** the Convention came into force internationally,

■ On **1 August 1998**, each maritime administration is to submit to IMO its intended programme for meeting the minimum qualification requirements for seamen sailing under its flag.

■ On **1 February 2002**, each maritime administration has to certify its seafarers in accordance with the new STCW requirements, and issue fresh certificates of the new stipulated models.

However, until 1 February 2002, maritime administrations may continue to recognise and approve a seamen's qualification certificate in two cases:

▶ when the training programme started prior to 1 August 1998

▶ for seafarers who entered active seafaring life prior to 1 August 1998.

Comparison between ISM, STCW and ISO 9002

An individual reading of these three reference documents could suggest that shipping companies are faced with puzzle, in which not all the pieces fit together. It is difficult to perceive any coherent whole.

The ISM Code covers safety and prevention of pollution risks, while the STCW Convention covers the competence of shipboard personnel, and ISO 9002, the quality of service (see fig 9.1).

Taken separately, each reference document might seem to require the

Comparison between ISM Code,

STCW Convention & ISO 9002 Standard

	ISM Code	STCW Convention	ISO 9002 Standard
Field of application:	Safety at sea and pollution prevention	Training, Certification and Watchkeeping	Quality assurance of services
Applicable to:	Ship Management Shipboard operation	Administrations Training Colleges Ship Management Shipboard operation	Contractual relationship between customer and supplier
Purpose: Demonstrate compliance with	The safety and pollution prevention requirements	The training, certification and watchkeeping requirements	The customers quality requirements
Means: Implementation of	A Company Safety Management System	A Company Crew Management System	A Company Quality Management System
Scheme of certification:	Shorebased audit: <Document Of Compliance> Ship audit: <Safety Management Certificate>	Company audit: <Certificate of Compliance>	Company audit: <Quality System Approval>
Validity:	5 years Subject to audit	5 years Subject to audit	5 years Subject audit
Compliance:	Mandatory	Mandatory	Voluntary

Figure 9.1

development of specific systems to meet specific requirements.

Seen from this standpoint, there is an obvious temptation to see the whole matter as a proliferating of constraints. Such a picture ignores the benefits for a company bold enough to venture into the area.

It has to be accepted that there are costs at an operational level, and a growing number of outside interventions, to check, survey, audit, assure and issue certificates that will require subsequent monitoring.

It is important to avoid an unnecessary duplication of activities that offer no real added value, or may even act as a brake on company growth.

How to integrate these new requirements? First a careful reading of the STCW Convention, concerning the company's obligations, shows that these are only the explicit requirements of the ISM Code in term of competence, qualification, training and records.

Second, the ISM Code and ISO 9002 are two separate entities which must not be confused. Does this mean that they cannot be reconciled within a more general approach ? Of course not, on the principle that it is impossible to speak of quality, unless a product or service offers all the conditions necessary to guarantee its safety in use.

In their essence the ISM Code and ISO 9002 are close to each other. However, the functions assigned to them and the results expected from them tend to keep them separate.

Links between ISM and ISO 9002
There are many links between the two standards. (Figures 9.2, 9.3)

■ Management responsibility is identified in ISO 9002 4.1. The authors of the ISM Code found it more practical to define such responsibilities in separate sections:

▶ Safety and environmental protection policy, corresponding to sub-chapter 4.1.1 of ISO 9002 (2)

▶ Company responsibilities and authority (3)

▶ Designated person(s) to be in charge of safety within the company (4)

Legend:
- ISO 9002 Standard only
- ISM Code and ISO 9002 Std.
- ○ ISM Code, ISO 9002 Std. and STCW Convention

ISO 9002	Safety management system	Safety & environmental protection policy	Company responsibilities and authority	Designated person(s)	Master's responsibility and authority	Resources and personnel	Development of plans for shipboard operations	Emergency preparedness	Report & analysis non conformities accidents and hazardous occurrences	Maintenance of the ship and equipment	Documentation	Company verification, review and control
Management responsibility			○		○							
Quality system	○											
Contract review												
Document control										○		
Purchasing												
Purchaser supplied product												
Prod. Id. & traceability												
Process control							○					
Inspection and testing												

Figure 9.2 links between ISM, STCW and ISO9002

Legend:
- ISO 9002 Standard only
- ISM Code and ISO 9002 Std.
- ○ ISM Code, ISO 9002 Std. and STCW Convention

ISO 9002	Safety management system	Safety & environmental protection policy	Company responsibilities and authority	Designated person(s)	Master's responsibility and authority	Resources and personnel	Development of plans for shipboard operations	Emergency preparedness	Report & analysis non conformities accidents and hazardous occurrences	Maintenance of the ship and equipment	Documentation	Company verification, review and control
Inspection, meas. & test equip.												
Inspection & test status												
Control of non confor. product												
Corrective & preventive action												
Handling, storage, pack. & deliv.												
Quality records												○
Internal quality audits												○
Training							○			○		
Statistical techniques												

Figure 9.3

▶ Master's responsibility and authority: the ship master is head of a floating small firm, active seven days a week and around the clock, distant from its base, with few stopping points (5)

▶ Resources and personnel: crews are no longer in fixed positions, and often consist of seamen and officers of different nationalities (6)

▶ Company verification, review and evaluation, with the obligation to oversee the ship operationally, regardless of its geographical location. Certain vessels return only very infrequently to their home port, and maintenance and checks on the condition of the ship may be carried out anywhere in the world.

■ Chapters 7 and 8 of the ISM Code (development of plans for shipboard operations and emergency preparedness) correspond to the following paragraphs of ISO 9002:

▶ Process control (4.9)

▶ Identification and traceability (4.8)

▶ Training (4.18).

■ Chapter 9 of the ISM Code (reports and analysis of non-conformities, accidents and hazardous occurrences), although it covers a wider field than ISO 9002, corresponds to the following paragraphs:

▶ Control of non-conforming product (4.13)

▶ Corrective and preventive actions (4.14).

■ The concerns of chapter 10 of the ISM Code (maintenance of ship and equipment) are divided up among the following paragraphs of ISO 9002:

▶ Inspection and testing (4.10)

▶ Inspection and test status (4.12)

▶ Identification and traceability (4.8).

■ The concerns of chapter 12 of the ISM Code (Company verification, review and evaluation) are divided up among six paragraphs of ISO 9002.

There are also paragraphs in ISO 9002 which are not covered explicitly by the ISM Code, because they are certification requirements:

▶ Contract review (4.3)

▶ Purchasing (4.6)

▶ Control of client-supplied product (4.7)

▶ Control of inspection, measuring and test equipment (4.10)

▶ Handling, storage, packaging, preservation and delivery (4.15)

▶ Statistical techniques.

Does this mean that a shipping company does not consider the contract review before committing itself to carry a product ? No, every ship is designed for a particular type of transport, and is classed as such by an independent classification society, with an international reputation.

Purchase and monitoring of equipment and installations are covered by maritime regulations, and are subject to inspection and monitoring throughout the useful life of the ship.

Rules exist to cover loading and unloading operations, as well as freight stowage and the ship's stability. The table shows how the two documents interact, even if their original purposes are different.

Management considerations

Here are the steps necessary for success:

▶ First, whether you are for or against these new reference documents, they have become unavoidable. If you do not agree, go to a gymnasium, write the names of the documents you most detest on a punch bag, and hit it as hard as possible until you are utterly exhausted.

The names will still be on the bag, as visible as when you started: proof that you cannot escape them. So, you have to learn to use them.

▶ Second, all three documents need to be analysed objectively, in order to find out what they have in common. This will help you avoid unnecessary duplication that can, wrongly, be seen as inevitable in these evolutionary approaches. The specific features of each reference document need to be identified. There are few, compared with what they have in common. These are often the points that lead to the issuing of a new reference document, to make up for shortcomings in an existing text. Unfortunately, hidden in an often confusing text, they hardly seem to justify this. Once identified, they are extremely useful, for they reveal the value, of the more abstract requirements of earlier documents.

▶ Third, a single system should be constructed from these reference documents. This is where the term 'Keep it simple seaman' (KISS) takes on its full meaning, helping avoid the traps and errors of faulty transposition, coordination, monitoring and updating of a company system.

▶ Fourth, responsibility for the system should not be entrusted to a single person. Remember Parkinson's Law, that any work expands to fill the time available for it. Unless you observe this law, the person will soon need deputies to do a job that, in fact, requires only person. Entrust coordination to a single person, and assign responsibility for the necessary action to each department manager.

▶ Fifth, do not delegate your own responsibility at the level of the system you have adopted. Delegate, by giving individuals the authority needed for them to assume their own responsibilities, within their own functions. Otherwise, sooner or later you will be faced with the consequences of Murphy's Law: the basic principle of which is that whatever can go wrong, will go wrong.

Back to the practicalities.

Why reconcile the ISM Code with ISO 9002?

Although the purposes of the ISM Code and ISO 9002 differ, it may be worth combining them in a joint approach, for the following reasons:

■ To strengthen company policy

Quality and safety have common roots. They represent requirements by the client. A product or service which does not offer a guarantee of safety in use cannot be regarded as a product or service of quality.

Although it is possible to talk of 'acceptable quality levels' (AQL), which may differ, depending on the clients requirements, such a term can no longer be used regarding safety of persons.

The fact of reconciling the ISM Code and ISO 9002 in a combined policy offers the advantage of approaching the delivery of a service with a single goal, namely satisfaction of the client. This goal combines quality and safety closely, in explicit terms.

■ To rally personnel around a joint project

In the first analysis, no one can be opposed to quality. Without clients, a company cannot exists. Employees must be aware of this.

Any success in reconciling quality and safety offers the advantage that, while quality primarily benefits the client, safety is for the benefit of company employees, enabling them to remain within the active workforce, as long as they are capable of coping with the task entrusted to them.

■ To avoid proliferation and duplication of documentary systems

'Procedure' is the word most frequently used in the ISM Code, and it comes second, behind the word 'requirements' in ISO 9002.

Investigation of these two reference documents shows that it is possible to draft joint procedures, and produce a single manual (figure 4.4).

Another advantage of combining safety and quality procedures is to reduce the number of such procedures, avoiding incompatibilities between texts intended to achieve common goals, and facilitating the tracing and updating of documents. Furthermore, it means that quality and safety are never dissociated when new documents are being prepared.

Comparison of the two documents, seen from this angle, reveals numerous links.

All items in the ISM Code are covered by ISO 9002, although they are not superimposed.

For example, operational procedures and contingency plans (chapter 7 and 8 of the ISM Code) are grouped together in paragraph 9 of ISO 9002 (Process control).

The comparison shows that ISO 9002 is wider in its application than the ISM Code. The code is more restrictive in its application, and does not explicitly cover the following factors:

▶ contract review

▶ purchasing

▶ purchaser-supplied product

▶ inspection, measuring and test equipment control

▶ handling, storage, packaging, preservation and delivery

▶ statistical techniques.

However, it gives greater importance to safety and the environment than ISO 9002, and in explicit terms.

ISO 9002 certification cannot replace ISM certification, or vice versa. Both approaches aim at complementary goals, the end purpose of which can be seen as:

'satisfaction of clients in the maintenance of a safety-conscious environment, for the benefit of the whole community'.

It comes down to a company policy decision. It is also a matter of common sense. Whether a company commits itself to ISM or to ISO 9002 certification, the effort needed to obtain both forms of certification corresponds to the many common links between the two reference documents.

The question is how to implement ISO 9002 in the maritime sector.

Certification of integrated systems

If each system is isolated from the other, the number of audits needed to prove conformity is bound to increase, as the reference documents progress.

This large number of audits can even militate against the very aim that is sought, safety at sea, in its most effective sense. Repetition of audits is bound to create such confusion that audited companies will be incapable of grasping the full implications of each, specific to a single reference document. They may even find contradictions among the reports issued by the various assessors. And this will be all the more likely because the requirements or different reference documents do in fact sometimes overlap.

For example, the ISM Code deals with many requirements relating to the competence of personnel on board. ISO 9002 also refers to this issue. However, the STCW Convention is clearly much more precise about such requirements than the ISM Code and ISO 9002 combined.

This is just one example. Areas common to all three reference documents. So it is a good idea to rethink the certification of such systems, giving up a sequential approach in favour of one based on balancing out requirements. This will make it possible to reconcile the idea of certification with a company's expectations of progress.

In order to achieve this goal, Bureau Veritas has developed a new approach, the aim of which is to integrate all these systems into a single certification operation.

Certification scheme

The certification scheme for integrated systems is quite straightforward. It comprises:

▶ initial certification for a period of five years

▶ maintenance of certification by means of combined annual audits.

Initial certification

Initial certification comprises four steps:

1: Company needs are analysed, to ascertain the scope of the systems to be taken into account for certification purposes. This information is used to draw up a single contract to cover all such needs, and then to programme the audits required to obtain the relevant certificates.

2: All these documents, describing provisions introduced by the company, are covered by a single document review, for the purpose of checking that they conform to the requirements of the selected reference documents.

3: Shore-based operations undergo an initial audit of company procedures. At this stage in the certification process, it is already possible to issue the document of conformity to the ISM Code.

4: Shipboard operations then undergo an initial audit, based on specific procedures for each type of ship. When the audit confirms that the systems employed meet reference document requirements, all certificates are issued together, for a five-year period:

▶ safety management certificate for each ship, under the terms of the ISM Code

▶ certificate of conformity of management for the company, under the terms of the STCW Convention

▶ certificate of approval of the company quality management system, under the terms of ISO 9002.

Maintenance of certification

Maintenance of certification is based on a similar principle, involving annual audits that cover all the reference documents adopted. This avoids any unnecessary duplication of such audits:

▶ onshore operations are audited annually,

▶ onboard operations are audited once, between the second and third year of validity of the certificates.

When the five-year period has elapsed, all certificates are renewed, following an audit performed on the anniversary date of the original certification.

Benefits for the company

The scheme displays many advantages in favour of the certification of integrated systems. There are major benefits for the company:

▶ there is greater flexibility in the choice and definition of the management system,

► integration of reference documents into a single system simplifies the documents involved,

► all selected reference documents are covered by a single contract,

► duplication of audits for certification and its extension is eliminated,

► all certificates are issued together, for a period of five years.

PART 3

Total
Quality
Management

Chapter 10
Quality as the cornerstone of a company's culture

There is no such thing as a difficult customer – just someone, like anyone else, who has particular needs. Your company must satisfy these: there is no choice – it is a matter of survival.

For all its insularity, Japan has grasped the importance of this. It has gained a sound reputation and a leading position in all the major world markets. This is no miracle. It is the result of common-sense policies based on principles of managing quality in every sense.

Management practices for the 21st century have to be based on supra-national regulations and agreed objectives. The western world needs synergy to start some recovery if it is to tilt the world trade balance in its favour again.

Companies have to attract customers with services that meet their expectations. They must inspire confidence and have a strong image.

Customers want services that meet their specific needs. Know-how, determination and positive action can provide these. Companies must abandon makeshift and individualistic ways of working in favour of shared knowledge and teamwork.

A company needs a new cultural framework. This does not mean embracing every passing idea and novelty but choosing the options for development and success with due vigour and discipline. It means researching into innovative ideas that are compatible with corporate policies, goals and work-force aspirations.

In shipping the customer is of course the shipper who wants cargo delivered safely and on time. In the majority of cases the shipowner is attempting to satisfy the needs of several different cargo owners who are using the ship to transport their goods.

This part of the book is primarily devoted to concepts and principles. For more specific applications on board ship see *Commercial Management for Shipmasters* by R L Tallack mentioned in the references.

It is not too extreme to say that awareness of customer targets must become an obsession. There are two principles that will provide the foundations for future prosperity:

■ Winning customer loyalty, by providing quality services

■ Making adequate profits for continual investment in product research and new efficient equipment while giving fair returns to shareholders, and fair wages to those who contribute to company success.

However this socio-economic approach would ultimately be incomplete and ineffective unless action were taken on an internal management level, to ensure similar personnel loyalty. Staff must be made to believe that quality service is the only acceptable way of managing a business.

Policy has to be thought out, primarily by considering its integration within the company. It is a question of determination: quality is the result of combined efforts and skills.

All involved need to find their natural place and assume their legitimate responsibilities, so that they will be individually committed, and responsible for their actions.

Clear actions

The company must be clear about the duties assigned to each department but also encourage ideas for stimulating projects, to be reviewed annually by the company chairman in person. These duties and projects should enable everyone to contribute according to ability, and assess their own contribution, in the context of team working.

All company departments need to be involved: sales, operations, technical, purchasing, finance, personnel, chartering, insurance and claims.

A chain of trust must be forged. Quality must become the cornerstone of a culture that will unite the personnel: having learnt the merit to work properly, they will want to do so. For such an approach to be successful, essential steps have to be taken.

Once the content of each job has been determined, it is vital to hand over responsibilities to the people performing them. This is a matter of motivation.

Competent staff are needed. Jobs are not created for individuals: people are hired to suit the needs of the job. This is no easy process, since human beings are not mere inputs in a system, but partners.

Staff training

Staff training is a way of making the work-force efficient, and keeping it so throughout the technological developments needed to improve quality. The company must also show concern for the personal development and fulfilment of its workers, in line with their aspirations and potential.

When these initial approaches have become everyday realities for the company, then comes the phase of attribution of broader responsibility, involving actual delegation of responsibilities, not just within the framework of the job, but as part of quest for individual fulfilment and motivation.

People are born with motivation: it is an inner force. Why not try and reconcile corporate and individual aims?

Delegation of responsibilities, such as the right to self monitoring, backed up by the creation of an environment that will encourage motivation, could release managers and experts from the cost-consuming duties of supervision and give them more time to assume their primary responsibilities of facilitating the work of those whose job it is to deliver shipping service.

The company must maintain this attitude by giving staff regular information at all levels, with proper attention to individual concerns. Rapid and reliable information will contribute to the action needed to prevent failures and errors.

Management participation

Another essential factor in the quality approach is management participation. This means setting an example. Employees judge managers not on their words but on their deeds. This is where they will decide how important quality is for their employer, and place it accordingly among their own priorities.

Those who have genuinely contributed to improve quality must be rewarded.

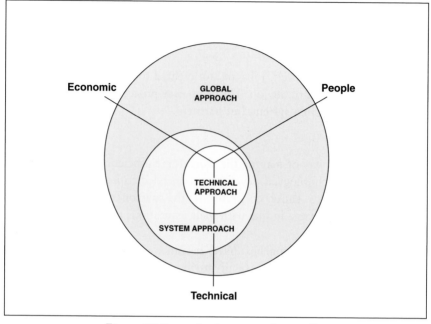

Figure 10.1 continuing quest for quality

Such incentives may take various forms. What matters is to mark an achievement, acknowledge it and make it known to all those contributing to objectives. No price can be put on recognition, which must be adapted to suit the individuals involved.

Succeeding quality concepts

This continuing quest for quality may be seen in (figure 10.1):

Economic: The company must make a decent profit in order to consolidate its achievements, make the investments needed for further expansion, and offer a fair return to those that show their confidence in it by investing in its future.

Technical: The ideas and creative energies which are reflected through innovation and the ability to offer new products and services.

Social: Every company possesses a human potential for creativeness, too long untapped, and in which it must invest for the future.

When quality assurance came into being, this new approach reflected the technical standpoint, with drafting of specifications for production processes and quality organisation procedures forming the quality assurance manual.

The whole approach used to be poorly communicated, and therefore misunderstood: and its lack of pragmatism and staff involvement means that it is still seen as an interference from outside, hence its failure in human relations terms.

And yet its strict procedures made a significant contribution to reducing the cost of faults and hitches.

A more recent concept is total quality management. It is based on human relations, and aimed at releasing the firm's creative potential by involving every sector of the personnel in improving quality. It is the attempt to achieve 100 per cent performance.

Total quality management

Within the framework of total quality management, the work-force must be trained before introducing self-monitoring as a way of giving responsibility to all staff. Internal quality auditing by company management must become a routine practice, even before quality circles are set up.

Staff agreement depends on management attitudes and commitment.

If quality is no concern of the bosses, why should it become a prime motivation for staff?

In order to assimilate this development, it is necessary to understand the basic concept of total quality management, which is based on simple ideas:

▶ A common definition of quality, accepted by the whole company. Why? The first defeat of our civilisation was the Tower of Babel, because the men building it no longer spoke the same language.

▶ Well-proven working methods, and suitable tools. Why? Having only a hammer as a tool means that all problems have to be solved will look like nails, even if you are an outstanding craftsman.

▶ A comprehensive and simple way of measuring quality, to help those who have to take action. Why? A runner who trains every morning needs to know his timing, if he wants to improve performance; this is just as true at work as during recreational activities.

▶ A recognised standard of performance, so that progress can be evaluated objectively. Why? Unless this exists, everyone will establish their own standard of performance, and divergences will create conflicts that have to be settled, instead of mobilising all the company's energies to achieve objectives.

▶ A means to recognise employees for outstanding contribution. Why? It is a basic need for everybody to achieve a challenge and a factor towards personal motivation.

This approach must be client orientated with the full participation at each level of the company. I remember one of my past chairmen who said: 'God gave us two ears and only one tongue, so that we must listen twice as much as we talk. You must have one ear for the client and one ear for the personnel. Both have good ideas for improving our performance.'

The customer
While travelling, I found a text in a restaurant that is worth considering when we talk about the client:

> 'The customer is the most important person in our business, whether he reveals himself in person, by letter or by phone.'
>
> 'The customer is not a nuisance, he does not interrupt our work, he is an end in himself.
>
> 'The customer does not depend on us, it is we who depend on him.
>
> 'The customer informs us of his wishes; we are never doing him a favour by listening, or advising him. It is he who does us a favour by offering us an opportunity to meet his needs.
>
> 'We have to help him define his needs and transcribe these, despite their full subjectiveness, in clear, precise terms in order to meet them.
>
> 'Everyone one of us, in every job and every department, has to do our work properly the first time in order to avoid delays and extra cost.
>
> 'A satisfied customer is our best advertisement; His satisfaction contributes to our brand image, in other words recognition of the know-how of our personnel.'

I have changed the wording slightly to make it apply to industrial and service firms, but, without being too longwinded about it, customer/firm relations should encourage the concept of service.

Travelling again

When travelling, I have met employers who tend to say:

'We would like to set up a total quality management programme, but our employees are not ready.'

In fact, that is not the problem: the employees are ready to follow management's example, if it is close enough to those engaged in the day-to-day business of promoting the company in the field.

The most serious obstacle is that the management is not approachable, and the management ego: 'we are the thinkers and they are the doers'. This attitude is wrong at a time when we have to mobilise all efforts to be competitive in a global market.

So when I meet an employer who is about to undertake a quality improvement programme, I ask him:

▶ Are you ready to write your firm's quality programme and make it known?

▶ Are you ready to set up the structure needed to improve quality, to meet changing market requirements?

▶ Are you ready to invest in training your personnel?

▶ Are you ready to take part in the project and listen to staff suggestions?

▶ Are you ready to inform personnel of the results and projects that will involve their future?

▶ 'Finally, are you ready to acknowledge the results of staff efforts to improve quality, and show your appreciation?

'Acknowledge' is a point that must not be overlooked. Every effort deserves reward: this is a basic principle of motivation.

Staff commitment depends on the attitude of management and its participation. The idea is: we are all involved in such a project, and security of employment depends on it.

The group attitude must be that of a single network of internal customer/supplier relations, culminating in the complete satisfaction of our outside customer. It is within such a relationship that the appropriateness of service to customer needs is defined in every link of the chain.

Chapter 11
How to implement a quality improvement programme

This chapter describes the content and the implementation of a quality improvement programme.

The quality improvement programme outlined may be tailored to the individual needs of any company. It is not expensive to implement. In fact, it will return substantial sums of money normally consumed by defects and errors.

This return will be directly proportional to the participation of the senior staff. And the degree of success will be directly proportional to the degree to which the general manager participates.

Investment can be minimal; the returns may be large. Savings during the first couple of years will drop straight to the bottom line, as they will be primarily the result of improved performance of staff.

The programme is self-perpetuating. After it has functioned for one year, you must evaluate the results, increase its scope and re-implement it. The improvement cycle is one of its ongoing features.

The 11 steps in this programme are:

1   policy statement

2   personnel orientation

3   quality improvement programme

4   quality improvement committee

5   quality measurement

6   personnel training

7   error-cause identification

8 objectives

9 corrective action

10 quality cost

11 recognition

1 Policy statement

Objective: Make clear where the president/chairman stands on quality. This first step consists of:

▶ defining the management performance standard

▶ integrating the statement inside the company quality policy.

Money may be wasted on defects and errors. Improper attitude, lack of attitude, lack of attention, and insufficient knowledge are the prime ingredients.

Management strives to control these situations. Often, however, we become too busy with 'managing the business' to give sufficient attention to the elements that cause mistakes. Reduction of error begins with an unshakeable management standard: 100 per cent performance must permeate the entire organisation instead of belief in 'what's good enough'.

This should be included in the quality policy. Everyone should understand that this is not simply a document to be placed in a book for executives; they must understand that it is a mandatory goal, and that anything less than systematic improvement toward that goal will be questioned.

An example of a policy statement could be:

> 'It is our policy to develop services and deliver products which constantly conform to the established requirements of our clients and to pursue the goal of 100 per cent error-free performance through formal management of quality improvement.'

This statement represents the general manager's commitment. It should be included inside the company's quality manual with the following:

> 'Accordingly, I have appointed a quality improvement committee to develop and implement a formal quality improvement programme. The committee will also function to resolve systems problems which require action across departmental lines. The committee will report directly to my office.'

2 Personnel orientation

Objective: Inform all personnel about the management standard for performance.

Everyone must understand that this standard applys at all levels of the company and in every area of the company business. This second step consists of:

▶ briefing management staff on the programme concept and intent

▶ obtaining their commitment to the programme

▶ mobilising the personnel on the company's policy.

The general manager should assemble his staff and inform them that he is launching a formal quality improvement programme.

The programme is in accordance with company corporate requirements that there be systematic quality improvement in every department. The staff should be informed that, along with mandatory quality improvement, the president has established a single performance standard that the entire company must strive to meet: that of 100 per cent error-free performance.

While it is understood that 100 per cent performance is difficult to obtain, we must continually strive for it. We should not accept defects or errors as normal in our business. We should understand that there will be mistakes, that there will be reversals. But we should also understand that we must immediately muster activities to correct these situations as they occur. Most importantly we, as management, should get angry when we see waste and rework, just as we get angry when a bank makes a mistake in cashing our check, or when an automobile dealer makes a mistake on a new car we've ordered.

Yet, for some inexplicable reason, we don't become similarly angry at the defective services which we produce or, worse yet, damaged products we ship to the client. Some managers believe that producing at a certain defect level is normal. There seems to be a dual standard: one of demanding error-free performance in our personal lives, and one of 'to err is human' in our business lives.

In shipping it is not always possible to organise complete excellence, masters do not employ stevedores and port services are in many ways not part of the system. However the aim must be to minimise loss and disruption and to follow up on any aspects of the contracts immediately. In this respect the Institute's book *The Mariner's Role in Collecting Evidence* can be seen as a corner stone in loss prevention measures. As an example see the tinted box which identifies the many items which have to be recorded when there is cargo damage.

3 Quality improvement programme

The quality improvement programme begins with each manager making it clear that there is no dual standard in the company. Everyone will strive toward error-free performance, and all management staff will question any performance that falls short of this standard.

While all management, from first-line supervision to the general manager, must participate to achieve significant quality improvement, it is the supervisor who ultimately contributes to the development of employee attitudes and practices in the offices and on the production lines: the supervisor is essential to successful implementation of the programme.

Why the supervisor? This staff level is just in between two levels inside the company. You could say that managers speak the language of money; while the work-force, the language of things.

Both languages use different vocabularies: but this does not hamper communication between management level and employees. Supervisors or at sea the boatswains or petty officers must be the 'bilinguals', able to transmit and explain the programme in a language that makes sense to employees and managers alike.

This is a critical element towards the success of the quality improvement programme.

The second step of the personnel orientation programme should be conducted when details of the operational programme are formulated by the quality improvement committee. At this point, a meeting should be called by the general manager and the committee chairperson to present the details of the plan to the management staff. They should be told how the programme will benefit them, how they will participate, and how they will be recognised for their efforts. It is essential to involve shipmasters and chief engineers in this process and to ensure that they involve the rest of the crew.

4 Quality improvement committee

Objective: Develop and guide the quality improvement effort to resolve systems problems adversely affecting management and service quality.

Since every department has the potential to make mistakes, each should participate in quality improvement. The degree of participation is determined by the situation that exists. The general manager should appoint a quality improvement committee large enough to encompass the major operating departments, but small enough to be effective. This third step consists of;

▶ defining the mission and the responsibilities of the committee

▶ selecting members of the committee

▶ establishing the practical organisational structure to reach the objectives of the programme.

The committee should meet monthly, as the situation dictates. It should not get involved in the treatment of non-conformities. Rather, it should concentrate on correcting the system which allowed the defect to occur. While the committee is responsible for developing and implementing the quality improvement programme, it is stressed that individual departments are responsible for developing their own detailed plans to ensure systematic improvements.

■ No additional expense

The establishment of the committee, and the implementation of a quality improvement programme, does not generally represent an additional expense. It usually only formalises and centralises what is presently happening in one form or another: often it results in the elimination of duplication. It is important to select the members of the committee carefully. It should include a mature member of the management team from each department: one who understands the need to improve and agrees with the

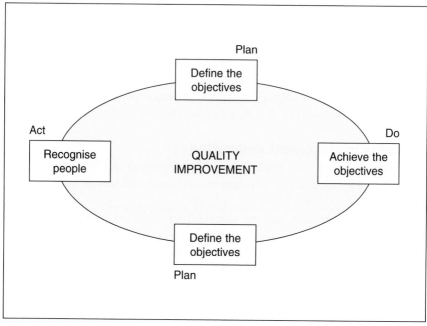

Figure 11.1 The management loops for quality improvement

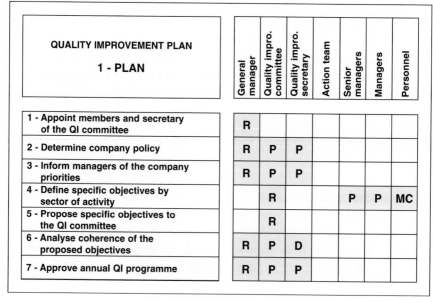

QUALITY IMPROVEMENT PLAN 1 - PLAN	General manager	Quality impro. committee	Quality impro. secretary	Action team	Senior managers	Managers	Personnel
1 - Appoint members and secretary of the QI committee	R						
2 - Determine company policy	R	P	P				
3 - Inform managers of the company priorities	R	P	P				
4 - Define specific objectives by sector of activity		R			P	P	MC
5 - Propose specific objectives to the QI committee		R					
6 - Analyse coherence of the proposed objectives	R	P	D				
7 - Approve annual QI programme	R	P	P				

Figure 11.2 Building a plan

Figure 11.3 Implementing the programme

QUALITY IMPROVEMENT PLAN 2 - PLAN	General manager	Quality impro. committee	Quality impro. secretary	Action team	Senior managers	Managers	Personnel
1 - Inform managers and personnel on the annaul QI programme		R	MC		P	MC	
2 - Launch QI programme in each sector of activity		R			P	P	
3 - Appoint leader for each action team		R					
4 - Organise action team according to specific objective		R			P		
5 - Define action plan to reach specific objective				R	P	MC	
6 - Perform specific action plan				R			

Figure 11.4 Making sure the programme works

QUALITY IMPROVEMENT PLAN 3 - CHECK	General manager	Quality impro. committee	Quality impro. secretary	Action team	Senior managers	Managers	Personnel
1 - Measure progress according to the objective				R	P	MC	
2 - Prepare monthly report by sector		R		P	P		
3 - Present monthly report to QI committee		R	P				
4 - Approve monthly activities report	R	P	P				
5 - Issue QI committee decisions report			R				
6 - Inform managers and personnel on results and decisions		R	MC	MC	P	MC	
7 - Measure results obtained for each objective				R	P		
8 - Present results to the QI committee		R		P			

QUALITY IMPROVEMENT PLAN 4 - ACT	General manager	Quality impro. committee	Quality impro. secretary	Action team	Senior managers	Managers	Personnel
1 - Communicate results obtained to managers and personnel		R	MC	P	P	MC	
2 - Provide effective recognition according to results	R	P	P				
3 - Recognise people who achieved specific objective		R			P		
4 - Put on hold action team activities according to schedule		R					
5 - Prepare QI programme layout for the coming year	R	P	P				
6 - Draft QI programme for final report		P	R				

Figure 11.5 Recognising people

concept of loss-prevention. Individuals should be selected who are not satisfied with the status-quo, people who are continually looking for improvement and recognition.

Committee members must be given authority to commit the respective departments to committee decisions.

The chairperson should be one who will be deeply involved in the total improvement effort, and who will have sufficient management clout to keep the entire quality improvement programme on schedule: someone who is constantly agitating for quality improvement.

The quality manager must be a member of the committee, but not the chairperson. The quality manager will be advocating quality improvement. Appointing another person in the chair automatically gets at least two people advocating quality improvement.

Further, with a quality manager as chairperson, the programme could be misconstrued as a quality department programme, which, of course it is not.

The quality department, in this case, should be considered a part of the total plant improvement effort, and its people utilised as technical advisors for details of the programme.

■ Formal quality improvement

The committee should develop its plan for formal quality improvement and present it to the general manager for approval and participation. Firm dates should be established for each step, and progress should be scheduled for review at certain general management staff meetings.

The elementary process for realisation of the programme is as follows:

▶ define the objectives

▶ achieve the objectives

▶ measures the results

▶ recognise people

Each step of the programme must clearly identify the sequence of actions to be undertaken and the responsibilities.

By way of example, figures 11.1–11.5 show the sequence of actions to be taken and the responsibilities for each stage of implementation of the programme.

Where: R: Responsibility
           P: Participation
           D: Delegation
           MC: May contribute

Each company, depending on its organisational structure, should define its own content within the context of its programme.

5 Quality measurement

Objective: Provide timely information on current and potential non-conformities in a manner that permits objective evaluation and corrective action.

The quality manager should obtain data from each measured area and present defect levels in trend format.

The quality improvement committee could list points at the operational level where they believe it would be beneficial to know performance in terms of defect levels. All ship audit, deficiencies and performance indicators should be reviewed against the list for reduction, expansion or modification.

Production departments are always measured and analysed. Service departments should also be measured. These include planning, commercial contracts inventory control, maintenance, stores, purchasing, bunkers and so on. These departments all have the potential for making mistakes.

Their errors impact substantially on profits, and since everyone can improve, the white collar areas should not be ignored. This fourth step consists of:

▶ identifying areas on board ships and in the office that need improvement

▶ measuring the actual situation

▶ reporting the results in term of progress, according to a schedule.

The use of a few strategically placed, easily understood, charts will contribute much to the performance, awareness, and improvement of operations and management alike. These should be placed where both management and workforce will see them, they should be sent to all ships involved in the programme.

They should always show at least six months of progress. There should be a goal line and an action line. The effort should be directed toward exceeding the objective. Should a problem occur, and the improvement trend reverses, it would become readily apparent when the results exceed the action line. Defect levels approaching the action line should trigger prompt management action to drive the results back in line with earlier improvement trends.

The charts should always identify the area being measured. This public display of performance measurement provides a psychological impetus toward improvement, as well as a practical corrective action tool. There should always be a way of showing how the gap between the actual and the objective can be closed. An example might be personal injuries to crew members.

■ Quality report

A quality report should be issued to management on a scheduled basis. It should convey, briefly and concisely, the problems, actions, and accomplishments of the reporting period. Major reports are issued monthly, and interim reports may be issued as frequently as the situation requires.

Each major report should contain a one-page overview which lists:

▶ areas needing general manager's attention

▶ significant problems and actions required or planned

▶ major actions accomplished

▶ the general situation

This overview should alert the reader to areas within the report that are of interest or must be reviewed.

Quality status reporting should clearly identify defect levels injuries, losses and trends. Reporting should identify, where possible, the cause of the most significant contributors responsible for, enabling management to take corrective action. The information must be simple and practical, to make the report functional as well as informational.

6 Personnel training

Objective: Provide to each employee an appropriate method and tools to improve their performance and to participate in action team.

The aim of the personnel orientation was to inform all personnel about the management standard and to explain them why it is important to implement a quality improvement programme in the company. The adhesion of the personnel to the programme is one other critical element for the success of the programme. This fifth step consists of:

▶ defining a simple problem solving method

▶ identifying the appropriate tool box see pp152-3

▶ teaching, through practical exercises, how to use the tools to fix a problem

■ Method

No one can treat any problem with indifference: the cost is too high. Particularly if the outcome could be a pollution incident. The problem must be approached with due deliberation, in order to find out and define the causes, and propose a realistic solution, before taking action eliminate it once and for all.

To be comprehensive, the method must provide for the action to be followed up, in order to ensure that the problem is finally settled.

■ Understanding the problem

Two situations may occur. Either there is a single problem, in which case it can be defined in a straightforward way. Or else, more frequently, there are multiple problems, which may not concern all members of the action team to the same extent. Here the team needs to agree on which problem to deal with first, so that teamwork will have its fullest effect. For example two ships may have had incidents one a collision the other a grounding. It is unlikely the causes are linked (they may be) but selecting the one with the most potential for improvement is probably the best way to start.

For purpose of this book, the second situation is taken as the starting point for the procedural approach.

▶ Identifying all problems of concern to participants: This step is recommended, since it enables everyone concerned to express his concerns freely, and make them known to other participants. This already represents acknowledgement by his peers which is a significant factor, not to be ignored.

▶ Obtaining information on problems: Not all information is available at the first meeting. When the problems have been expounded, it may be advisable for members of the action team to seek additional information, before deciding which problem will be dealt with by the group. Such an approach avoids the possibility of ignoring a problem which may be important but which, for lack of information, might be overlooked by a majority of participants.

Information should be factual, preferably with figures wherever possible.

Before making this final choice, the team examines all available information. This approach allows the way in which certain problems have been expressed

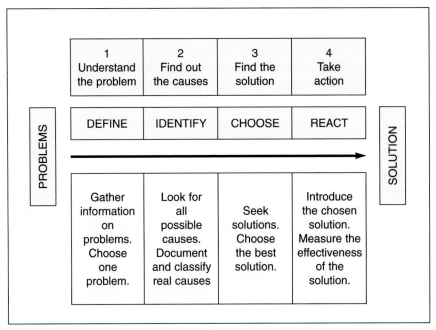

1 Understand the problem	2 Find out the causes	3 Find the solution	4 Take action
DEFINE	IDENTIFY	CHOOSE	REACT

PROBLEMS → SOLUTION

Gather information on problems. Choose one problem.	Look for all possible causes. Document and classify real causes	Seek solutions. Choose the best solution.	Introduce the chosen solution. Measure the effectiveness of the solution.

Figure 11.6 Problem-solving method

to be confirmed or shown to be inappropriate, and so lets the group see things more clearly, when taking the next step in the method.

▶ Choosing the problem: As the selection process continues, the problems brought forward by each member are struck off the list, and this continues until a single problem has finally been chosen. This final choice should be made on the basis of democratic principles accepted by all participants. A charter, stating the principles by which the group operates, may be useful from the beginning, and provide a reference at all times. This is particularly helpful when, in the heat of the moment, passions run high among members of the group (see fig 11.6).

By means of successive selections, the number of problems regarded as most important by the action team is first reduced to no more than four or six, so the problem regarded as pre-eminent by the group can ultimately emerge.

The choice is the culmination of a consensus, based on understanding of the problem, but also on mutual respect among participants.

■ Knowing the causes

Once the problem has been chosen, the most difficult part begins. When faced with a problem, everyone tends to jump to conclusions, and put forward his own solution. This is a trap to be avoided, since a quick solution could prove unsatisfactory, and the problem might have to be re-examined later, when energy and enthusiasm may have flagged.

The only real solution is to start by looking at all possible causes.

Looking at all possible causes: There are three possibilities at this stage in the method:

▶ The team is aware of the real causes of the problem, in which case it can move directly to the search for and choice of a solution

▶ The team believes that it knows the causes, in which case it investigates the presumed causes before beginning to look for a possible solution.

▶ The team has no clear idea of the real causes of the problem. In this case, it must examine all possible causes, by collecting facts and information that will enable the real causes of the problem to be identified, by answering the following queries:

> Where is the problem observed?
> At what point in time does it appear?
> Under what conditions does it occur?
> Why? What happens?

Another way in searching for real causes is to define the problem and its causes in terms of 'is/isn't' situations. For example, the problem occurs during such a period of time, on such and such a day, but not during other periods, or on other days.

As to the investigation progress, possible causes should be tested and vetted. Although methods/tools are used, commonsense and intuition should not be forgotten; qualities that can sometimes have surprising effects when the team cannot make progress.

■ Documenting and classifying real causes

Reports on possible causes are established from the answers obtained during investigation of the problem. One should always be ready to go back and reexamine the sources, if the information available is inadequate to define the real causes properly. Such information can be used to outline and visualise all possible causes. A simple visualisation of the problem and its causes can be more telling than endless descriptions.

▶ Classification of causes, in decreasing order of importance, shows the sequence in which the group should examine them, until the problem is eliminated. This visualisation is in itself a way of initiating a plan of action. At this stage in the method, the group agrees on the real causes. If the team cannot agree, it must take the time needed to understand the problem, in terms of detectable effects and causes. It is often a simple question of communication, comprehension, or even inattention. Reformulating the problem and its causes can help maintain the group cohesion that is so vital to the success of the project.

▶ Circumscribing and investigating the problem: By this stage, the group has identified the problem and is aware of its real causes, but no solution has yet been proposed. There may be several possible solutions, and only one of them will be adopted. The immediate question is what to do in the meantime to neutralise the problem's effects? So, the most realistic temporary solution needs to be found, on the basis of:

the problem's seriousness: its extent, consequences, cost and implications,

urgency of the situation: deadline, constraints, available time,

how the problem has developed: is it diminishing, stabilising or increasing?

■ Finding the solution:
If the action team has followed the steps recommended in logical order, it now has all the data needed to begin the search for a permanent solution to the problem.

The chosen solution may be a measure that will remove the real causes. Taking action against an assumed cause is ineffective: the problem will recur sooner or later, or bring about other problems of a different kind.

Remember the image of the inquisitive person who opens a can of live worms: the only solution he can find in his panic is to empty them all into a larger can, to prevent the worms from escaping. It is a way of blocking the problem; but it is not a solution.

All possible solutions have got to be identified, for each of the causes defined. Some creativeness is needed at this stage. Every member of the team has to be completely free to express as many ideas as possible.

When the team is faced with difficulties, it should have no compunction about calling upon an expert for advice. His role is to answer the participants' questions, and help throw new light on the problem.

The group may be considered to have completely this creative phase when it has at least two valid solutions to compete with each other.

▶ Choosing the final solution: Again, the team has to decide between two or more options.

A choice based solely on a vote may be sufficient for simple problems, requiring only minimal expenditure, which can be absorbed directly by the budgets.

When the problem is complex, a more rigorous approach is needed. The team has to compare options with one another, on the basis of selection criteria, or even combine certain options, in order to achieve the most effective solution, both technically and economically.

When the problem requires large investments that have not been budgeted for, the action team prepares a dossier to back up the implications of a suggested solution, the schedule for action, and the cost involved in carrying it into effect.

This final point is most important: any quality effort forms part of a continued quest for progress, which should lead to improve performance and efficiency in the company. This means that any investment has to be justified before any action is taken. Blocking the problem is no more than a temporary solution, while awaiting the decision to introduce the final solution.

You should not wait too long before taking action, otherwise the participants ready to take the programme on, will become disheartened.

Applying the chosen solution: Once the project has been accepted, its introduction may be entrusted to the same group, or to dedicated teams.

The plan of action provides for organisation of the project: what needs to be done, who is to do it, when it is to be done, where, how etc.

The direct involvement of the action team in implementing the solution is another form of acknowledgement that should not be ignored.

Some changes are still possible at this stage: another problem, concealed during investigations, may even be discovered. The same action team should preferably follow the project to its conclusion.

Monitoring and measuring the effectiveness of the solution: This is the ultimate phase of the method. Members of the team check that the solution is providing the expected result, through monitoring over a period, and measurement of effectiveness solution the conclusion.

■ Toolbox

At the beginning of this chapter, the problem-solving method was presented step by step, describing the actions needed to achieve a permanent solution. The right tools for such actions now need to be sought. (See pp152-3)

Many tools are available. It is only by using what seems appropriate that you can learn their practical usefulness, so identify those most suitable to you. So it is time to discover them, and choose the ones that make up the group's toolbox.

A tool should not be rejected out of hand just because it seems neither too complicated or too elementary. Each has its advantages and drawbacks. Some can even help release a situation when the group seems to be at a dead-end.

All the tools discussed in this chapter will be of the greatest help in moving a problem towards its final solution. However, never forget that common-sense must take priority.

■ Action team

Using tools in an unmethodical way is like building with a blindfold on. Method becomes necessary when two or more people are working together on the same project; and it is essential for any group with a common goal.

Tools are only means to an end, and the method is no more than a guide to conduct. The result depends not only on members' individual abilities. It is based on the conviction of the team, its determination, its cohesion, and also

TOOLBOXES

Brainstorming – An organised group session to obtain the widest number of ideas concerning a problem and its causes and to find potential solutions to this problem.

Check sheet – A pre-format document to collect information on the problem and to identify its causes.

Simple vote – A technical term used for the pre-selection of the problems to be treated by the group.

Weighted vote – A technique used after the simple vote to select the first problem to be treated by the group.

Graph chart – A visualisation of a data to show results of the corrective action: pie charts, bar graphs, pictorial graphs.

WWWWHW – A technique used to covers all aspects of a problem and its causes: What? Who? Where? When? How? and Why?

Causes-effect diagram (or fishbone diagram) – A visualisation of the problem and its causes grouped under headlines such as: ship, people, methods, equipment . . . to identify areas where improvement is needed.

Pareto diagram – A graph based on rule 80/20 is used to classify data in decreasing order of magnitude to orient the corrective action.

Flow chart – A visualisation of a process, step by step, used to identify where the problem may occur.

Is-isn't logic – A technique used to clarify the information about the problem: It is, it is not versus: We don't know.

Multi-criterion diagram – A matrix based on criteria to facilitate the choice of a solution among few possibilities.

GANTT diagram – A network of activities required to achieve the objective in time.

Logigram – A flow chart critical step that identifies logical solutions proposed to achieve the objective.

Farce diagram – A visualisation opposing the causes of the problem and proposed solutions to solve it.

Decision tree – A visualisation used to compare solutions which are mutually independent in terms of result.

Arrow diagram – A network of activities required to achieve the objective in time. It is possible to identify the critical flow of the project from this visualisation.

Cedar diagram – A dynamic visualisation of the cause-effect diagram where actions and results can be posted in the area where the group works.

on acceptance of the proposed solution by those who will be most directly affected by its consequences.

There are three factors in favour of a team approach:

▶ a solution, if it emerges from individual investigation, is often seen, however, brilliant it may be, as a kind of 'carpetbagger' solution, and it attracts resistance to change. The time gained in drawing up a solution in splendid isolation could be lost later in trying to persuade those concerned of the benefits of the proposed solution.

▶ more can be done, faster, by working in a team. In a project nothing is straightforward, and a greater number of activities can be carried on simultaneously.

7 Error cause identification

Objective: Provide personnel with a vehicle for communicating errors and problem situations to senior management for action.

One of the most difficult situations that employees face is management-employee communication. This programme will provide an unique vehicle for communication. It will ask employees to identify problem areas without having to supply a solution to the problem. This sixth step consists of:

▶ identifying the possible roots of the problem

▶ providing the means to inform the management for taking action on the recognise problem.

This programme is different from a suggestion programme in which the employee is required to know the problem but also to suggest a solution. The error cause identification (ECI) programme is successful on the basis that an employee need only recognise a problem, management is responsible for finding the solution.

Asking employees to describe problems that cause errors is strong evidence that management is committed to the entire quality improvement effort. If management then acts towards defect-free performance, the employees will do their part.

Experience shows that over 90 per cent of the items submitted can be acted upon, and fully 75 per cent can be done at the first level of supervision. Frequently, first-level supervision is left to do the best it can in producing defect-free services, in spite of serious obstacles left in its way by the senior staff. This programme is designed to provide a place on the management's agenda for operating problems which cause significant waste, along with the routine meetings and reports, customers and telephone calls which so rapidly consume management time.

Employee communication in this programme saves money: since the line employee or seafarer is a profit centre generating savings every time the job is done better or quicker.

The error cause identification step should operate under the direction and the guidance of the quality improvement committee.

8 Objectives

Objective: Engage all personnel in a continuous quality programme to improve the global performance of the company.

Each year the general manager should review the strategic company plan and fix objectives for commercial and operational sectors. It is good management practices to pave the road for the future.

The objectives of the quality improvement programme are different. They are based on non-conformances observed during the daily operation, and which need corrective actions to meet the policy statement concerning the improvement of the company performance. This seventh step consists of:

▶ defining the opportunities in terms of objectives for the company

▶ preparing appropriate action plans to eliminate non-conformities or to improve existing practices.

The content of the programme should be based essentially on management priorities. Each department of the company should identify an area where they can contribute to the expected progress. At this level of the organisation an action team should be created with the participation of seastaff and office personnel.

The result of these activities must be to encourage/permit individuals to propose specific objectives for themselves and their groups.

The specific objectives proposed by each action team must be reviewed by the department manager, master or chief engineer. The proposed objectives must be compatible with management priorities.

All objectives approved by the committee will constitute the annual quality improvement plan of the company.

Proposed objectives must be presented in a formal way to be approved by the quality improvement committee (figure 11.7).

The objective must be measurable, realistic and under the direct responsibility of the department that proposed it.

It must describe:

▶ the reason for the objective

▶ potential saving for the company

▶ how the result can be measured

▶ the intended action plan to reach the objective

QUALITY IMPROVEMENT PROGRAMME		N	
Objective:		Key compo.	Key system
		Department:	
Cost investment:			
Action plan:		Why? Potential saving & how to measure the result?:	
Decision of the committee:			

Figure 11.7 How to present a project for quality improvement

▶ an estimation of the cost investment to solve the identified problem.

To gain support, the departmental heads should identify two keys which fit with the management priorities:

component key: performance, delay, cost, service, safety, environment

system key: management, people, procedures, ship equipment, market (client requirement or legal constraint).

9 Corrective action

Objective: Provide a systematic method of permanently resolving problems on a timely basis.

Corrective action is the 'payoff' step. It closes the loop of the quality improvement programme and clearly fulfils the responsibility of contributing to the profits of a company. This is most successful when it operates on the 'Pareto' principle which states that the most important should be attacked first.

Problems must be identified, classified as to importance, and formally resolved. This eighth step consists of:

► implementing the corrective action

► auditing the process to validate the efficiency of the corrective action.

A successful method of corrective action is to establish three levels of constant activity, as follows:

► short regular meetings should be held on board ships and in head office and to examine the problems detected and to prevent recurrence. Major problems should be documented on an item action log which lists the problem, its impact, cause and responsibility. These meetings are productive only when identifying and removing the cause of defects are the key issues of the meeting.

► monthly, or special meetings should be held by the general manager and his staff to review problems with overdue resolutions. Usually items reaching this level need senior management decisions. Items requiring complex or long-range action may be assigned to a task team.

Beyond a corrective action item log, a formal corrective action notice system should be maintained.

► when an undesirable condition is noticed, a verbal corrective action request should be issued,

► when verbal corrective action requests are not complied with, a condition notice should be issued which indicates that verbal attempts at obtaining corrective action have been ineffective and a formal notice is necessary

► a corrective action notice is sent to the department manager or ship when all else has failed to generate corrective action. This form requires a written reply from the department manager as to the corrective action taken on the discrepant condition and the person who failed to heed earlier notices

► the receipt of a corrective action notice should be a serious matter. Appropriate reprimand to those failing to heed earlier requests to correct discrepant conditions is in order. Any individual collecting a series of corrective action notices should be brought to the attention of senior management for appropriate remedial action.

The corrective action item log, the discrepant condition notice, and the corrective action notice should be in pre-printed form.

10 Quality cost

Objective: Quantify the cost of error and the cost of activities necessary to prevent, appraise and remedy error as a means of reducing the total cost.

While there is no simple definition of the costs of quality, the following definition is established for the purpose of understanding the wide scope of activities which may be chargeable to quality costs.

The quality cost to a company is the difference between the actual cost of making and selling services and the reduced cost, if there were no possibility of failure of the services or errors by the people in production, sales, or use of these services. This ninth step consists of:

▶ measuring major quality costs in the company

▶ analysing the actual situation

▶ identifying area of potential saving for new quality improvement.

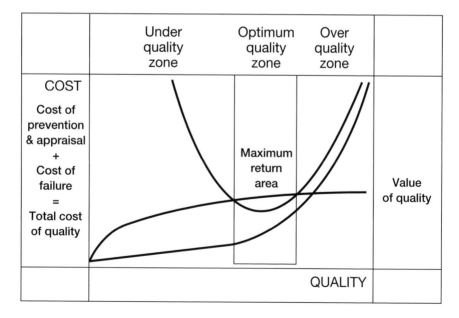

Figure 11.8 What is the real cost of quality in your company

The cost of quality is its only practical measurement (figure 2.18). It has long been said, 'if you can't measure something, you can't control it'. The most practical and meaningful measurement is still plain, old-fashioned, bottom line money. Where quality is concerned, we are talking about the costs of error.

All the elements contributing to this cost may be segregated into three categories:

▶ **Prevention costs:** incurred in an effort to reduce failure costs and consequent appraisal costs

▶ **Appraisal costs:** the costs of inspecting, testing, analysing and auditing the service to determine its conformance to requirements

▶ **Failure costs:** resulting from the failure of the service to conform to requirements during production.

However restricting quality costs in this manner is parochial. Quality costs should be construed as any costs relating to mistakes, defects and failures made by anyone in the company which hamper its operation. Now we have taken account of errors from the ships into the offices where the most far-reaching and costly errors occur.

> A wider definition should be: 'The quality cost of a company is the difference between the actual operating cost and the operating cost if there were no failures in its services and systems, no mistakes by its staff, and no possibility of failure or mistakes'.

For most companies, this wider definition would result in much higher quality costs than in the more restricted definition; and much higher values in ratios, quality cost to sales. A wider definition is important because it indicates the much larger possibilities for improvement available to the company by application of quality control principles than would be realised from the restricted definition.

All costs of quality figures must be compiled by the controller and reported regularly.

A quality cost report should indicate and clearly identify progress in the following areas:

▶ a quality cost summary reflecting actual, versus planned, derived from the controller's cost of quality report

▶ the basic quality measurements showing service conformance for all operating areas over a period of time

▶ major problems affecting quality cost, outlining the responsibilities and the plan for improvement

▶ cost reductions achieved by ships and head office departments, showing monthly and year-to-date savings.

This report should be addressed to the general fleet manager.

Corrective action can come from many departments, but the figures have to come from accounts. Analysis will provide a practical management tool to identify problem areas by cost priority, provide justification to corrective action; and help recognition at all management levels for contributions to profit through quality improvement.

To explore the practical aspect of quality cost, please read Annex 2 of this book.

11 Recognition

Objective: Provide employees with recognition for those who participate.

Employees who continually strive for quality improvement, or who are instrumental in effecting significant cost savings, should be recognised for their contribution. This serves as a reward to the contributor and as evidence that superior effort is encouraged and appreciated by the company.

Recognition is a fundamental need for everyone. Studies show that people place recognition for their efforts among the aspects of employment they value most. The most effective type is one that is lasting and increases esteem among associates. A cash award is welcome, but generally soon forgotten. A certificate, presented by the general manager with the employee's associates present, will be long lasting and appreciated. This tenth step consists of:

- defining means to both recognise significant results and also for participation

- awarding personnel so as to stimulate new participation in the quality improvement programme.

As previously stated, it is important to emphasise that this recognition should, generally, not be in the form of money, prizes, or trinkets. Except in unusual circumstances, the employee is simply doing better what he was hired to do anyway.

Of course, if someone saves the company a large sum of money, a financial reward might be in order. It should not be considered a routine measure, however.

The type of recognition will differ from one company to the other. There is no strict rule, but I suggest that you read Annex 3 of this book. You may be surprised by the result of this study. Keep the recognition programme flexible and in the character of the company. For improved stimulation, the recognition awards should be sparse but meaningful.

Chapter 12
Quality and safety at sea: the human element

Quality and Teamwork

Teamwork is an illusive concept and it has many facets. The sailor's aphorism of 'all pulling on the same rope together' is one example of physical team work and the sea shanty helped to keep movement consistent and in time.

In most organisations today this image of teamwork is inappropriate because production or the provision of services depend upon many people contributing different operations to achieve an end result.

To some extent the analogy of the sailor's rope now becomes the company objective or mission and the teamwork element comes from a willingness to contribute to company performance.

There is another difference between teamwork viewed as a physical attribute, and teamwork seen as an intellectual activity. When team work is recognised as an intellectual activity, improvement in performance becomes possible because people can use their creative abilities to initiate better working practices, efficiency in production processes, superior design and more attractive services.

The company which can tap this creative source of improvement in a committed and constructive way is going to be more competitive in the long term than one which is unable to do so.

Before the full effects of real teamwork can materialise two important elements of management must be present. First, the culture in the company must be right and the work force rewarded for working as a team. Secondly the company must possess good team leaders.

Team Leaders

The team leader has a vital role to perform which is complementary to the line or operational role. Some of the qualities which are required can be worked out by considering what has to be achieved. Leaders must be able to provide:-

- ▶ A sense of direction and clarity of purpose

- ▶ Communication keeping everybody together

- ▶ A positive attitude in support of company objectives

- ▶ Critical but constructive appraisal/assessment to provide meaningful feedback on performance

- ▶ Re-enforcement of roles making sure that the contribution of all members of the team is valued by the team members

- ▶ Proper reward and recognition for team effort

- ▶ Respect for the individuals in the team by representing them well with other departments

The role of the chief executive

So far we have looked at sailors pulling on ropes and managers getting their work done through teamwork and team support. The concepts are related to actual teams carrying out tasks in a company context. However any organisation which is divided into departments has the potential for inter team rivalry which, if not managed well, can be very destructive.

It is the role of the chief executive to ensure that teams within a team ie the company can perform to best advantage. They too must demonstrate leadership and show commitment to policies and practices which encourage participation.

In a study reported in the UK Royal Society of Arts in 1996 the key elements of world class companies indicated that they are successful in promoting a culture in which teams can operate in the following ways:

- ▶ They plan and organise their own day-to-day activities and carry them out with little or no supervision

- ▶ They support each other and arrange their own cover for absence, overtime, training etc

- ▶ They measure their own performance in terms of output, quality and costs

▶ They discuss and agree their own targets and work towards them

▶ They report performance to their manager as required

▶ They plan and organise their own improvement activities

▶ They identify and arrange their own training and development needs

▶ They liaise with other teams and support areas where necessary

▶ They seek constantly to improve their skill levels, processes, methods of working facilities and overall performance

▶ They communicate well both within the team and with other teams, areas and managers

▶ They operate autonomously to achieve the objectives set by their manager.

Here we see the evolution of a mature organisation, reaching towards the limits of capability, in which the qualities of innovation, renewal and team work supercede operational practices and routine administration.

The next step is, of course, to envisage two like minded organisations sharing a complementary role in the market place; and that in theory there is no limit to the number of organisations and teams that can be linked together if they are mutually self supporting and quality minded.

Unique characteristics of shipping companies

Shipping companies are unique in the way they have to manage fleets of ships. Each ship in both autonomous and yet part of the company. The fact that decisions have to be taken on board without continuous head office intervention means that the task of building company ship teams is that much more difficult.

Clearly the sub contracting of different crews for each voyage may keep crew costs down but this strategy does not enable continuous improvement to take place.

To understand more fully the complex interaction between sea and shore staff I carried out a survey to explore the differences and values between command and management.

Every ship must have a command structure to ensure a rapid response in emergencies. However we must also be realistic. Emergencies occur only rarely and when they do it is usually because of bad management. The two are closely associated.

One of the interesting conclusions from the questionnaires was the fact that on board ship personnel are expected to carry out the job that relates to their rank or position.

These ranks and positions are reinforced by certificates of competency in the deck and engine departments, so reinforcing job titles.

When it comes to leadership and team building it is clear that in many shipping companies the managers now see it as their role not to do anything more than ensure the right certificates are assigned to the people in the appropriate jobs on board.

These managers have invariably been certificated too and carry with them the shipboard culture where it is not expected to think outside the boundaries of their job role.

Some companies have, however, broken with tradition and are achieving steady improvement through a different approach to management. It is this approach I want to discuss in terms of human behaviour.

The human element

The ISM Code is due to come into force in June 1998. To meet its demands there are four types of resources available to maritime transport companies:

▶ management

▶ people

▶ ships and equipment

▶ organisation and systems

Because all companies can buy ships in the open market, management and men offer the key to success today.

In the maritime transport sector, human error is mentioned as a factor in

90 per cent of collisions at sea, and in 75 per cent of shipboard fires and explosions.

Aviation catastrophes have also been caused by human factors:

1991, *Agip Abruzzo,* carrying 80,000 tonnes of light crude was struck at night while lying at anchor off Livomo, Italy, by the ro-ro ferry *Moby Prince*. The ferry caught fire and 143 persons died. The fire on the tanker lasted seven days and moderate oil pollution affected a wide area of coast. The collision resulted in legal action in the italian courts and declaration of limitation of liability by the owner of the *Moby Prince* on the ground sof crew negligence. Claims totalling about $50m have been presented against the owners of the *Moby Prince,* whereas the limit of liability will amount to about $4.4m.

1994, a Royal Air Maroc ATR crashed 35km from Agadir. The captain, whose last words were 'Die, die . . .', apparently wanted to commit suicide, thereby causing the death of the forty passengers and crew members (Cause of accident: despair caused by an unhappy love affair).

1996, *Sea Empress* stranded off entrance to Milford Haven, UK, when entering port. Bad weather made refloating difficult and 65,000 tonnes of oil leaked into the sea and caused grave damage to highly sensitive coastal areas and to fishing.
The aggregate value of claims are likely to exceed those connected with the *Braer*. The ship was eventually floated and taken into harbour where remaining oil was transferred to other ships.

1996, a collision, in India, involving a Saudi Boeing 747 and a Kazakh Illyshin II 76, caused the death of 351 people. (Cause of accident: language error – poor language skills of one of the crew).

If this random unpredictable type of human error is to be avoided it is essential that the individual takes responsibility for his own actions. To be safe the individual must understand the limitations under which he is working, and because it is easy to make mistakes, he must be willing to have his actions verified and checked either by himself (a vital habit) or by somebody else (good management). See The Nautical Institute book on *Bridge Watchkeeping* to understand ways of developing the habits of monitoring and self checking.

Why is the human element so important? The answer is because aircraft and ships are moving. They are intrinsically unsafe in so far that if the pilot or the navigator operating alone were to have a heart attack and die the aircraft would crash and the ship would run aground or cause a collision. This is the fundamental difference between transport and manufacturing. In transport the vehicles are moving and at all times they have to be safely controlled.

To control a ship reliably at all times individuals need to draw upon the following human characteristics.

■ Knowledge:

This is the individual experience and skill, by which an individual obtains a recognised qualification or certification, providing access to certain positions of responsibility.

■ Will:

This is the determination and desire to do and succeed in an undertaking. Without willing, knowledge remains a necessary but inadequate condition of success.

■ Power:

This provides access to responsibility and authority for action. This parameter is not dependent on the individual, but on the style of company management.

To find out how people at sea and ashore felt about their work, I conducted a survey, using the three key motivational factors listed above.

What quickly became apparent was the difference in perception between sea staff and shore staff about the relevance of the human factor in safe ship operations: consequently, in many cases management were adopting practices which were detrimental to achieving the levels of safety they themselves set as desirable.

The survey was carried out over a six-month period and it produced 109 answers to the questionnaire that had been distributed to companies in Belgium, Croatia, France, Greece, Italy, Kuwait, Malta, Morocco, Spain, the United Arab Emirates, United Kingdom and United States.

The answers were analysed, and the findings classified under two separate headings:

A – Officers with ten or more years' experience at sea

B – Shore-based managers, or officers with fewer than five years' experience at sea.

Members of **group A** may still be at sea, or currently occupying a management post ashore. Some also had prior experience of command on board ship.

Members of the **group B** were either seagoing officers at the start of their careers, or managers who have never held command on board a ship. The absence of acknowledged seagoing experience was a particular point of interest.

To emphasise the differences in viewpoints between the groups, we deliberately ignored officers with six to nine year's experience at sea. The analysis thus covered the attitudes of these two groups.

This concerned the whole company work-force, ashore and onboard ship.

The three parameters of knowledge, will and power interacted directly with ability (doing) and behaviour (being).

Synthesis of overall analysis
'Knowledge, will and power to do'

When a situation allows these three parameters to be combined, conditions are ideal for the work-force to be able to meet the tasks assigned to it. This is the minimum level to be expected in a company: a competent and responsible employee, who performs his tasks with enough independence to be efficient.

The overall analysis shows that conditions are very satisfactory for officers and managers as a whole. Opinions are more divided about crews and onshore workers. According to **group A**, weaknesses exist at the level of the ability and wish to carry out high-quality work. For **group B**, the situation was considered quite satisfactory.

'Sociability, will and power to be'

The combination of these three parameters, in addition to those associated with professional ability, enable an employee to go beyond the minimum expected level of competence. In order to be effective, the competent employee must be encouraged to develop as a team member. This involves the behaviour needed for social integration within a team.

The overall view reveals major differences in opinion between the two groups. For **group A,** this type of behaviour evolves. *None of the parameters mentioned were at a sufficiently high level for crews to develop effective teams, and officers did not have the power to provide a remedy.* According to **group B,** the overall situation was satisfactory, except for the behaviour of onshore workers, which could be improved.

'Ability, will and power to have done'

These three parameters illustrate the capabilities and behaviour of an officer or manager in performing the duties within a company: a professionally competent manager who is also able to lead a team.

The overall analysis reveals very great differences of opinion between the two groups. For **group A,** *the main weaknesses were seen to lie in the lack of know-how of all officers and managers in motivating employees and creating cohesion within teams.* The group also believed that officers did not at present have the power to take action in this area. According to **group B,** the situation was very satisfactory for all company employees, whether seagoing or onshore.

First conclusions

The overall analysis reveals that it is not a matter of two structures confronting each other about the problems of risks involving the human element, but two different worlds of experience:

▶ officers with experience at sea

▶ officers with no or insufficient experience at sea

Officers with experience at sea regard the situation with a more critical eye, while those lacking such experience tend to extrapolate the situation they are familiar with and apply it to the whole company, without any real distinction between onshore and offshore activities, hence the divergence of viewpoint.

Analysis of the survey findings suggests that, despite differences of opinion between the two groups: There is a serious problem at the lower levels concerning the competence of both crews and onshore workers. This problem, affects teamwork and is tending to induce a degree of carelessness, which also affects certain officers:-

The feeling of frustration expressed by officers concerning this ability to develop effective teams also exists on shore, but it is less evident in the results.

A lack of genuine delegation of authority may account for part of the frustration expressed by officers.

You may consider that a questionnaire designed to test attitudes to work is not the best way to identify weaknesses in the human element. However we know that teams which are well lead and which contain well trained personnel are more effective than personnel employed simply to carry out a job and fulfil a role.

Everybody has the view that ships crews are good teams because they represent a physical unit and the ship generally arrives safely with the cargo in fact. A careful study of Mr R L Tallack's book *Commerical Management for Shipmasters*, also published by The Nautical Institute, reveals that there are wide differences in voyage accounts between a well run ship and a badly run ship.

So if a shipping company wishes to raise the level of performance of the fleet a number of key decisions will need to be taken.

Recruitment

In any company success is a combination of all the skills needed to achieve good performance. Selection criteria need to be carefully defined and qualifications vetted before anyone is hired.

It may also be necessary to offer certain inducements, in order to attract the best recruits. These are not only pecuniary: working conditions, the state of the fleet, company image and other benefits should be taken into account.

The 1978 International Convention on Standards of Training, Certification and Watchkeeping for Seafarers (STCW) has been undergoing amendment, and the revised version was published during the third quarter of 1995.

This is a step forward in helping shipping companies. However, it will never replace the recruitment selection process used by the company, which has to answer the question of whether a particular individual can, or cannot be integrated into that company. The most highly qualified are not necessarily the most cogent members of a team.

Maintaining skills

Initial training should focus on company policy and procedures: These must be practical and relevant, which is not often the case at present. As proof, read a procedure used within your own company, putting yourself in the place of the person who has to act on it. If it is not well written you will soon understand the whole problem.

Recruitment of good people is one thing; maintaining them is another. Time is an eroding agent, causing wear and tear not only on equipment, but also on people. It is vital that companies keep their personnel up to date and encourage them to keep on developing.

To do this a constant vitalisation process is needed, by means of in-house and outside training wherever possible, with application exercises at operational level. It is not a question of conditioning, but a person must be ready to act and react in every particular situation. It may be a matter of survival. A well-trained workforce is the best assurance of preventing risks. Encouraging membership of a professional association is a good way to raise levels of awareness.

Integration of the workforce depends on training, lack of which was emphasised by participants in the survey. It is often assumed that training for certificates of competency is all the training needed for seafaring. This is a great mistake. Teams can only exist in a team environment and companies must carry out their own team building.

Trusting officers

Officers consider that they possess the right skills, but that management does not leave them the freedom they need to exercise their command properly. Special training might be needed to fill the gaps revealed in answers to the questionnaire.

The questionnaire also reveals the desire of officers to take responsibility-but some individuals do not feel ready to face this, in an environment that has evolved too quickly for them.

This finding confirms the previous point about maintaining skills. The discrepancy between new and existing capability must be narrowed as much as possible.

A higher level of trust should enable new styles of command to evolve in which delegation empowers every individual to take on responsibilities and the authority needed to assume them.

Delegation should not remain a matter of mere intention, since intentions have no ultimate effect. It must be recognised that only freedom of action can create action, and therefore progress.

Overhauling structures

Learning and applying new relevant skills are the minimum actions to be expected in any successful organisation. Even then, it is important to understand the goals being sought, and for individuals to feel involved and useful as members of a team if they are to achieve fulfilment.

Success involves going beyond the level of comfort. Set habits need to be re-examined critically, and more efficient ways of working found, in order to make the company's position stronger in relation to competitors.

A corporate project may be one solution to consider, as part of a continuous improvement in quality and safety.

This approach can provide incentives for the reappraisal of behaviour, in order to create a team spirit, integrate individuals skills into a shared project, and rally the chosen group around common goals. But this implies the need to prepare officers and managers for such an assignment.

Such an approach ranges beyond the framework of certification. It is based entirely on the human element, acknowledging its value, so enabling action to be taken with greater freedom. The ideas expressed by officers with extensive experience at sea were not the sign of any forthcoming mutiny, but a warning cry, which cannot be heard on land, once the ship has crossed the horizon.

The roles and responsibilities of ships' officers and crew are hierarchic and in a sense comfortable. Everybody knows their place and the orders go from top to bottom. In so doing there is little room for initiative, little sense of participation in decision making and limited scope for creating the conditions for high levels of motivation.

What this questionnaire has discovered is that individuals enjoy a challenge, they respond positively to empowerment and the opportunity to work as a team. How this change of culture is to be achieved can be seen from the analysis of the questionnaires which dealt with personal attributes and in particular competence, teamwork ability and management.

Competence of personnel to do the job

Personal skills, at the level of work performance, are based on the following:

▶ Knowledge which is defined in terms of understanding and the ability to perform tasks. This know-how depends on training, and recognised work qualifications. Without appropriate qualities, the individual is incompetent so leading to occupational risks.

▶ Will to do one's work properly, which depends mainly on man's inborn need for acknowledgement, which contributes to personal motivation. In order to develop a team, an interest must be displayed in every individual. Without such effort, individuals will tend to drift-apart.

▶ Power to assert oneself professionally in one's work which is based on the acknowledgement and delegation of recognised responsibilities. It does not depend on the individual, but on opportunities offered by the company for his professional fulfilment. Without such opportunities, the individual can suffer a feeling of misunderstanding, which can be in reflected a sense of frustration.

When an individual is understood, accepted and acknowledged, the gates of job satisfaction open, culminating in the person becoming a professionally competent employee.

Ability to work in a team

A professionally competent person does not guarantee success, when he is engaged on an assignment where safety depends on his ability to interact with other people. Skill is an essential, but insufficient factor in preventing such risks.

So one must transcend technical skills, and aim for integration of the individual within a coherent and efficient team. This result may be obtained through the following sequence (see also figure 12.1).

▶ *Sociability*, can be defined as the social skills necessary to work together, and a readiness to communicate freely and exchange opinions with other members of a team. It is the minimum needed before one can speak of motivation within the work situation. Without such sociability, the

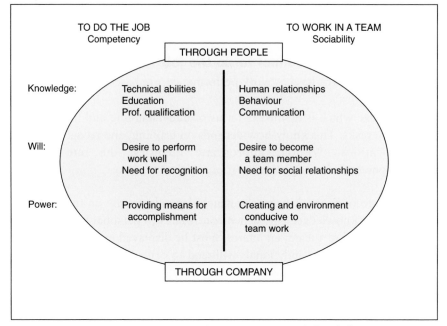

Figure 12.1 Personnel: competence and durability

tendency is towards indifference and loneliness, which makes it impossible to build a team, and prepare it for any eventuality.

▶ *Wish to become a responsible member of an efficient team.* This wish depends not only on professional skills, but above all on the vital need of human beings to have human contacts, in or outside the work situation, with other people who understand them. Such relationships help overcome solitude and remoteness. They help him create a human environment, where he can put down roots and enjoy a sense of brotherhood, when he feels the need. Without this wish and conviction, the individual can move into isolation, and develop an unsociable character, which reinforces his isolation and incommunicability.

The possibility of living as a team, sharing one's own joys and difficulties, as well as others', creates a team spirit. This is essential to morale and positive action on difficult situations. It does not depend on the individual, but on the conditions created by the company, in which a team can be forged, and loyalty created, not with a view to a job or salary, but for the pleasure of continuing to work together. Without such opportunities, a person cannot express himself properly in his solitude, and is bound to become discouraged.

Persuasive power of management

The role of a manager is to make arrangements for the assignment given to him to be completed. He must lead by example. People work more easily for a competent manager who shows respect for his staff. When they have doubts, they are reserved in their efforts. When they trust a manager, they are ready to follow, regardless of the difficulties inherent in a task or assignment.

Management know-how must embrace managerial skills towards superiors, but also leadership and attitude towards the workforce. Personnel mobilisation and efficiency depend on the leadership skills and style of managers. Without such know-how, the performance is bound to suffer.

The wish to lead a team and to succeed is based on the need for recognition and a sense of personal achievement. To succeed, the sense of achievement must transcend the individual. It must be shared with his team. Coaching them towards a goal involves clarity of purpose and recognition of results. He has to listen to his team, understand and give support, so that they can succeed together. Without this readiness on the part of a manager, the change needed to ensure corporate improvement cannot be carried through successfully. Such an attitude blocks any search for progress, by maintaining the status quo.

Provisions introduced by company's senior management to bring about change. Such change must take the form of evolving management practices. Change should make it possible to broaden the field of responsibilities and authority, through successive delegation. Such delegation does not represent any loss of personal power: It is a necessary step, if each individual is to be able to contribute effectively to progress within the company.

A cultural change is involved. Such a change cannot not be provided to order, it must be a matter of trust. Without such an opening, management styles remain rigid and authoritarian. This is the initial brake on progress, contributing to demotivation of managers, who feel no responsibility for decisions imposed on them.

If the management style is open it becomes participatory and 'mobilising'. This is the first step towards real progress. It also helps motivate managers, who feel jointly responsible for the actions taken. Nothing is black or white, everything is movement forwards or backwards. It is a matter of choice. This indispensable cultural change is the best guarantee of progress.

Achievement of change

Achievement of change is initiated by company senior managers, but it is not confined to their directives and expectations. Change emerges from a consensus to which everyone must contribute.

Personnel, whether managers or subordinates, must obtain the necessary competences, both technical and human, to accomplish the tasks or assignments given to them. This provides know-how.

Company senior management must create an environment and favourable conditions in which personnel can achieve fulfilment, and encourage participation, as part of a genuine delegation of powers. This provides power to act.

Involvement and an ongoing consensus between the leaders and their teams provide motivation and mutual expectation of all participants.

Extending the capability of the company.

Once a company has achieved a high level of performance it can seek new relationships with outside organisations. For example the oil industry has a long tradition of partnerships, either sharing in the exploitation of an oil field or the sub contracting of energy transport to recognised companies.

Chapter 13
The missing link

Quality is a fascinating and disturbing topic, an unavoidable rite of passage, and companies are having to re-learn its significance, sometimes in a most painful way. Every theoretician champions his own methods. However we must go back to the natural theory of evolution, for it applies to all systems.

What is quality?

This question too often remains unanswered and unanswerable for so many managers, probably because of an instinct for self-protection, or the habits born of long professional experience.

Until the recent past, quality meant the conformity of a product to its specifications. In other words, any item produced in conformity to pre-established technical criteria was regarded as a quality product. Any deviation from the specification raised a problem of conformity, which had to be handled in the least expensive way for the firm.

The question that may now be asked, with hindsight (which is always easier) is whether a product that conforms to its specification a quality product?

Of course, if I ask the question in this form, the answer is bound to be double-edged: perhaps it is, perhaps it isn't. Such an answer is no help at all, although it may cast doubt on the definition.

This is what has happened with the changing demands of users of products and services. Doubt has led to discussion, and this has produced a new definition of quality.

■ In this new definition, quality is the adequacy of a product or service for the real present and future needs of users.

And this has the ring of truth: what is the point of conformity to a specification if the product or service is not sold? Every one of us can quote at least one example of a product that conforms to its technical specifications, and which has proved to be a commercial flop.

So, we have to go beyond the idea of technical conformity, and extend it to all needs, which go well outside the technical framework. This is what we call 'adequacy' for needs.

Adequacy can in turn be defined as a perfect relation or equivalence; something appropriate which corresponds perfectly to its purpose, and is therefore suitable, and adapted.

Although I do not want to get into philosophy, Spinoza considered that truth lay in the adequacy with which thought corresponds to reality, and that error was merely a gap in our knowledge.

The term adequacy is therefore fair and truthful, since it means nothing more or less in relation to present need. Adequacy, because it is not enough to meet the needs of the present, we must discern how needs will change, not only in time, but also in space, as constituted by a multi-patterned market, where niches remain to be won.

Quality today therefore represents a company's openness to its customers, in terms of readiness to listen, and responsiveness. We no longer create needs, in order to be useful. We have to understand and anticipate needs, so as to move ahead of our competitors and win market share.

We cannot achieve this to the expected quality unless we work at it, all together, with a single goal; satisfaction of all our customers whatever their differences. Naturally, it would be easier to make only a single high-performance product. Easier also for our suppliers, but would it be appropriate for all our clients?

If we do not succeed, purely for reasons of efficiency, our customers may find the answer to their needs among competing firms. And every one of them will be right, for this is how we behave in our private lives, for our personal benefit. Decisions taken by our clients are not fundamentally different from our own decisions. It is up to us to recognise this and draw the right conclusion before it is too late.

And why not total quality?

This is where the problem arises: quality has for too long been misused in terms solely of conformity to a specification, and the definition still remains deeply rooted in our culture.

Technical quality is only one gauge of quality among many others, such as availability, delivery, price and the service provided. Latest surveys in countries with a market economy show that service, for instance, is an increasingly important factor in the final decision to purchase a product, of which shipping transport is a key element.

Total quality reflects a company's ability to respond effectively to the multiple needs of the market. The total quality outlook is that of a leader, an organisation and resources concentrated on providing the right response to the changing needs of every shipper. If such an outlook is short-term, there can be no talk of total quality. Many cases of such short-sightedness are reported in the press, and they have deplorable effects on the country's economy, and also on the morale of those who still strive to succeed in business.

So let us look at total quality, and see what this means in practical terms. There are two possibilities at present:

■ a quality assurance programme

■ a quality improvement programme

Each of these options has advantages, but also drawbacks:

▶ a quality assurance programme represents a strict approach, requiring documents in evidence, when contractually required by a customer. On the other hand, if followed properly, it minimises risks of error,

▶ a quality improvement programme represents adaptability, and leaves a wide margin for creativity. The risk is that unless such creativity is mobilised around carefully channelled and targeted projects, it can be a source of wasted energy.

So, which programme should be chosen? Before taking any decision, let us look at key factors in each programme.

Integration logic

The main aim of a quality assurance programme is to achieve control of the quality system, and obtain assurance that it is functioning properly, in relation to a reference document which the company has announced its intention to observe.

In order to maintain such assurance, two factors in the programme are essential:

■ internal quality audit, planned and initiated to schedule

■ periodic system review by general management.

These two operations may be enough to show that the system is under control, or that there are discrepancies between practice and the reference document. If such deviations are observed, suitable corrective action is taken to restore the system.

In fact, a reading of the ISO 9002 Standard shows that the very spirit of the text is a contractual relationship between purchaser and supplier or subcontractor. In the standard the 'supplier' refers to the company concerned by the quality system. There is therefore a contractual obligation, imposed, acceptable or accepted by the firm supplying the product or service, in relation to quality, not easy to communicate to a supplier, who must also be regarded as an economic partner.

All means are therefore deployed to control and assure quality, on the basis of acknowledged commitments.

The main aim of a quality improvement programme is the better overall performance of the existing system. The intention is not to make the system more sophisticated, but, on the contrary, to simplify it whenever possible, and improve its efficiency.

To achieve progress in this area, two active methods of participation may be used:

▶ annual quality improvement goals, planned and followed up in accordance with a schedule

▶ voluntary suggestions expressed by the employees throughout the year.

Both these actions may help improve the system, not because there are non-conformities in relation to a reference document, but because the work-force feels concerned by the need to achieve progress for the company, which assures the future of individual employees, in the face of competition.

When this motivation exists, it cannot be maintained unless the efforts of those involved are fully acknowledged.

This voluntary approach relies on the conviction of people, but it also requires a shared vision of the future by the whole management team heading the campaign. This is what I see as the flexible aspect of quality, requiring a constant readiness to listen on the part of management, and a degree of transparency that will silence the rumours which interfere with personal initiative.

All means are therefore deployed to improve and advance quality in all parts of the firm.

Each of the two programmes offer undoubted benefits for a company:

▶ in the first case, assurance of the quality of proper functioning of the system

▶ in the second case, permanent improvement of the system.

Once this has been understood, there will be more readiness to accept the need for both programmes to be linked for the greater benefit of the firm. Even then, thought must be given to integrating them in an evolutionary quality approach, since any system that fails to change starts moving backwards.

In the quality improvement programme, the intrinsic motivations of the individual are made to contribute to the total quality programme. The quality assurance programme provides confidence in the system, and its continuance is ensured through an awareness that all ideas for improvement are valued.

Knowledge and control of the system through the quality assurance programme therefore, in turn, becomes a vital source of information to guide the quality improvement programme.

Both programmes, from this viewpoint, form part of an operating logic that is vital to any total quality programme, where constraint and flexibility can blend together satisfactorily.

It is from the links between these two programmes that the total quality management programme will emerge, on a level above both of them.

Total quality management (TQM = QAP + QIP)

Total quality is obtained from these two programmes:

- The quality assurance programme (QAP) is used to control company processes, and reassure customers that they will obtain a product or a service which meets their needs. This may be shown by certification.

- The quality improvement programme (QIP) is an approach that tries to aim for excellence, by eradicating mistakes and faults and looking for new working methods that will improve performance and efficiency within the firm.

Although both programmes are positioned differently within a total quality management approach, there are points in common:

▶ management participation

▶ establishment of a quality policy that emphasises the importance of quality for the future of the firm

▶ training of the workforce to obtain the means needed for such a policy

▶ setting of goals to remove causes of errors through corrective action

▶ current quality indicators, to monitor progress achieved, and focus on new goals.

The key elements of quality assurance are:

- A permanent organisation with clearly defined quality responsibilities.

- A quality manual stating the rules of the organisation and the responsibilities of individuals which refer to a recognised reference document

- Procedures for saying who does what, when, where, how and why

- Efforts concentrated at the level of operational control in accordance with the quality assurance system adopted by the company, to ensure services and operations are carried out in accordance with procedures

- The use of statistical aids to validate data

Internal audit and external audit to check that the system is working properly, and that recommended provisions have been adopted.

In short, this is more a technical approach, the aim of which is to ensure the service is provided consistently with the minimum errors and omissions.

The highlights of quality improvement, compared with quality assurance are:

- The organisation is adapted constantly to suit situations, ideas and goals

- The progress plan, to which the company is committed is reviewed regularly

- Efforts are concentrated on the quest for excellence in all parts of the firm.

Conclusion

It is no longer a matter of asking what difference there is between quality and total quality. Quality relates to the product or service, and total quality to the means deployed in order to succeed.

It is no longer a matter of asking whether one should assure quality or improve it. Both are needed to succeed. But (there is always a 'but' in the answer to a question of such importance for the future) in what order should one proceed, since one cannot improve something that one does not possess? So the system has to be created, before it can be improved. Quality assurance is the first step, total quality management the second, the quality improvement links one to the other. It will then be possible to say:

Total Quality Management enables a company to do things right.

Annex 1: Technical

How to write a procedure, simply

Whatever code or standard is chosen as the reference against which a management system is to be measured, the term procedure is paramount. In the ISM Code, for instance, the word 'procedure' represents 20 per cent of the keywords used, while in ISO 9002 it represents 17 per cent.

These figures, intended to do no more than illustrate a situation, reflect the importance that standardising bodies attribute to procedures in documentation.

What is a procedure?

By definition, each procedure is a document describing a specific activity in the planned system, and states the responsibilities and means required to obtain the expected result.

A good procedure is a document that is complete in itself. It should be drafted in a form accessible to the person who is to use it. Too often, I find companies using cumbersome, even incomprehensible, procedures which no reader would want to read beyond the first page.

Three years ago, I carried out a survey of the expectations of users of procedures. More than 70 per cent of those questioned had not read the whole document, or even admitted that they filed them away without reading them. Reasons given for such a situation include:

lack of time

illegibility of the document

amendments not shown clearly (involving tedious cross-checking of two texts)

'pen-pusher' procedures, remote from day-to-day realities.

Compared with these dispiriting views of procedures, users are unanimous in considering that the two primary qualities they seek in a procedure are usefulness, and easiness to understand.

For administrative staff and managers, the third quality is ease of updating their procedures manual. For those in the field, the third quality is the practical usefulness of the content for the purpose of the work to be done.

These reactions can be used to improve the function performed by a procedure, provided that the author agrees to expound the subject in clear terms, and take account of user's expressed needs.

If the procedures are well written, they should combine to define company know-how, and contribute to the overall efficiency of the system. Quality of service, safety and prevention of pollution risks need to be documented in clear, usable and practical procedures.

One often forgotten advantage is that well written procedures can constitute the documents needed for staff training. A company that can write its procedures doe not need a training manual, but only teaching guides, for the purposes of its training plan.

The question that remains is – how to produce a good procedure.

Writing a procedure

In fact, a procedure is not so much written as produced, after its structure has been devised and visualisation completed. These are not idle words, but practical commonsense, intended to allow procedures to effect the changes they are bound to bring about.

Napoleon claimed that: 'A picture is worth more than a thousand words'. He was right, and it is even truer today, with all the communication problems that arise in modern companies. Some practical method is needed, to avoid longwinded, rambling documents that exhaust their readers, instead of stimulating them to action.

The method proposed here is intended to remove superfluous text from such documents, and give priority to visual means.

Assessment of whether a procedure is needed or not: When the code or standard states that a procedure is required, there is no possible doubt, and it must be provided. Otherwise, the appropriateness of a procedure has to be analysed, on the basis of the likelihood of errors and their consequences:

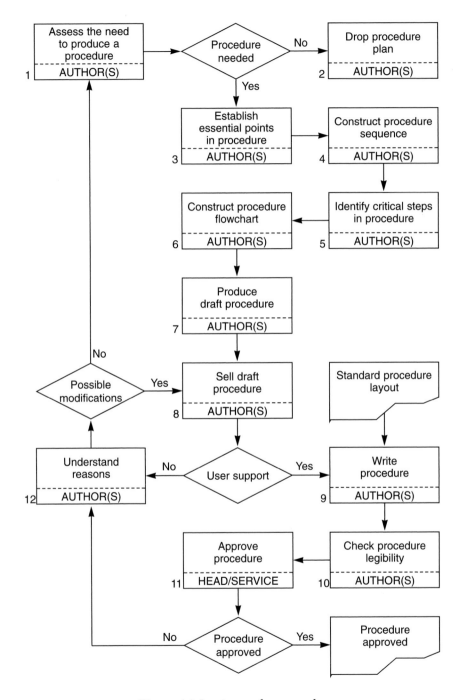

Figure A1 Logigram for procedure

If there is no risk, a procedure may not be necessary.

If there is a risk, it is preferable to initiate the process of the production of a procedure.

Establishment of key points in procedure: These are the points that need to be covered by the procedure, and which are necessary to its understanding.

Construction of procedure flowchart: Key points are classified in chronological order. In the flow chart, fig A1, boxes indicate 'steps' and arrows indicate 'paths' towards achievement at the expected results.

Steps are rewritten, beginning with an action verb and the function, or unit, responsible for the action stated above appears in the lower part of the box.

Identification of critical steps: Critical steps are those in which a situation, or particular condition, generate two possible answers. The path is altered depending on the answers.

Construction of procedure logigram: The introduction of such situations or conditions change the path into a network, showing retroactions and the documentary resources needed (eg forms, data-banks).

Drafting the procedure: The logigram is not enough in itself. Wherever necessary, essential additional information must be included for each step, in the space provided for the purpose (eg 'not later than 15th of each month'; 'cf Appendix 2, Specimen form'.)

Words should be simple, and sentences brief. The logigram and text must make the subject clear and reassuring for those who will be using it.

Selling the draft procedure: A product without a customer is completely useless. A procedure without a user is equally useless. It is important to obtain the support of those concerned by implementation of the procedure. A change in old habits is seldom welcome. Will the procedure improve the lot of the client in the department concerned, or will it merely be another apparently useless administrative obstacle?

The author of the procedure has to put on his salesman's hat, and use his powers of persuasion.

If the backing of users is not obtained, the reasons must be sought, to see whether modifications are possible

If such modifications are possible, the project must be resold to users

If modifications are not possible, the relevance of the whole procedure must be re-examined, which means going back to the very start.

Writing the procedure: Once the project has been sold, the procedure needs to be written in its final form, complying with the standard layout adopted by the company.

Checking procedure readability: This is the final step, to ensure that the terminology and style used in writing the procedure are appropriate to the level of understanding of users. Methods now exist for measuring this quantitatively.

Approval of procedure: In a participatory approach, approval of the procedure should be delegated to the head of the department in which the procedure is to be applied. In a centralised approach, approval of the procedure should be the responsibility of the manager of the departments involved.

In either case, the person responsible for approval must check that the procedure properly meets his client's needs:

▶ Approval means that the particular system possesses a procedure documenting a specific activity,

▶ If approval is withheld, the reasons must be sought, to find out whether modifications are possible.

The lengthy written description given here reveals the obvious advantages of the logigram: without visualisation, the text would be even longer. Once the method of drafting a procedure is formatted, the accompanying text can be reduced to its briefest expression.

However, brevity does not imply the exaggerated use of abbreviations. On the contrary, they should be avoided, and any that are used should be explained clearly in the 'terminology' section of the procedure.

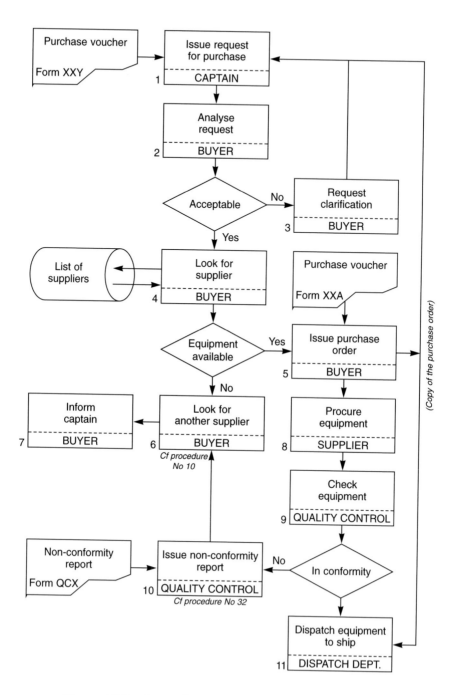

Figure A2 Logigram for purchase of standard equipment

Figures A2 and 3 illustrate a practical example of the procedure for dealing with a request by a ship's captain for equipment.

Box number:

1. Complete purchase request, using form XXY.

2. When information on the purchase request is unclear or inadequate, clarify the situation by radio, mentioning this radio message on the form (3).

5. Listed supplier: state contract conditions on order voucher (price, delivery date, conditions of reception and payment).

6. Unlisted supplier: look for a supplier and report the situation to the captain.

9. Equipment delivered at Head Office and in New York is inspected by the quality control department. Any other equipment delivered in another port is inspected by the first mate.

10. If a non-conformity is found, a non-conformity report, is issued within twenty-four hours of receipt of the goods. It is sent to the purchasing department by fax.

WHERE?	PLACE OF DELIVERY
Quality control department:	Head Office and New-York
or	
First mate on ship:	Ports en route

11. **NB:** no equipment delivered to Head Office or in New-York can be dispatched to a ship without the agreement of the quality control department. In an emergency, only the superintendent can authorise dispatch of the equipment, with specific instructions to the ship's captain for its inspection.

Figure A3 – Procedure for the purchase of equipment

Practical considerations for procedure visualisation

The advantages of presenting any procedure in the form of a logigram seem so obvious, for reasons of simplicity and ease of understanding. However, reducing a complex subject to a simple visual form calls for considerable efforts at analysis, reflection and synthesis.

A good visual layout should:

Cover the subject, starting with one practical component and culminating in another practical component, and deal with only one subject at a time. The flowchart should provide an answer to a precise question asked by a user. Company procedures, as a whole, form the combined transferable know-how of the company, in the form of an answer to the question 'How?'.

Fit on to an A4 page; otherwise, the subject should be subdivided in simpler steps, to make them practical and applicable.

For assessors, for instance:

The first logigram might explain how someone becomes an internal assessor

The second logigram might explain how an auditor becomes a confirmed assessor

The third logigram might explain how an assessor becomes a lead assessor

The fourth logigram might explain how to maintain assessor status.

This structure provides simple expression of something complex but necessary.

Avoid any crossed arrows in the logigram. If two lines do cross, there is a very high likelihood of error (cf Murphy's Law). With a little imagination and experience, the components of the logigram can be rearranged to avoid any possibility of error.

No more than five symbols should be used. Whenever a new symbol is used, it makes the logigram harder to understand, and introduces doubts. The American expression 'KISS' (Keep it simple, seaman) takes on its full meaning with regard to the global outcome being sought.

The best way to define the framework and avoid omissions is to preform the procedure requiring documentation.

Practical considerations for procedure presentation

For a procedure to be complete, a congenial framework has to be provided for the logigram and accompanying text. This is the procedure environment. It has two aspects:

Administrative, for the cataloguing, approval, issue, classification, amendment or filling of a procedure

Structural, to standardise layout, in order not to leave anything out.

Administrative aspects

The procedure must state:

company name

title of procedure

procedure number

revision index

date of revision

page-numbering

names and signatures of author and approver.

The positioning of each factor mentioned above must be established in advance, so that users can find the same type of information in the same place from one procedure to another.

Structural aspect

In addition to these administrative factors, information in the procedure environment has to be given a structure. The items making up this environment are:

■ Purpose

This states the reasons for the existence of the procedure. In general, they define stipulated requirements and methods to be employed to control a process.

■ Scope of application

This items shows who is concerned by this procedure within the organisation.

■ References

This item refers to internal or external documents concerned with the application of the procedure.

■ Terminology

This item should contain only definitions specific to the subject involved, and the few abbreviations used, to facilitate understanding.

■ Procedure

The logigrame and text should occupy two pages, facing each other, so that all necessary information can be found without turning a page. This is the core of the procedure.

■ Identification and filing

This item should states clearly who is to retain the required information, in what form, and for how long.

■ Documents

There are many different appendices to a procedure. They contain all the details that would make the actual procedure top-heavy, but which are needed to accomplish its purpose in full. They provide practical examples, making it easier to understand how information should be circulated within the company. All such information, when placed in an appendix, can be revised more easily, without altering the text of the procedure itself.

To summarise, a procedure should be laid out as follows:

Purpose, scope of application, references and terminology.
Logigram.
Accompanying text.
Filing and references to appended documents.
Appendices, where necessary.

Procedure readability

A procedure is no use unless users apply it. An obvious thing to say, but how many people take the time to check?

Checking in the field is too late. It needs to be done earlier on, before the procedure is sold to those who will be using it every day. This is the author's responsibility, not the users'.

A method is needed for this. There are several, the simplest of which would seem to be the 'Fog Index'.

The method is as follows: Take samples of approximately 200 words, beginning and ending with a complete sentence. Count the number of:

words (W1)
sentences (S)
words of three syllables and more (W3)

Determine the level of understanding F1, by means of the formula:

$$F1 = 0.4 \, [W1/S + 100 \, (W3/W1)]$$

The average result for all text samples should not exceed 10, and no individual sample result should exceed 12.

This is one method among many. The aim is not to measure anything, but to ensure that the procedure can be understood by those who have to use it.

■ Conclusion

At first sight, the method of writing a procedure as outlined in this annexe may seem longer, since it requires careful thought all the way through the production sequence. In fact, it draws attention to the essential questions, for which an answer must be found, before a new procedure is implemented.

It is a practical exercise, which avoids time-wasting and unnecessary frustrations:

▶ It allows constructive dialogue as soon as it is produced, since the sequence of actions becomes logical

▶ It makes auditing easier, since the activities covered by the procedure become more transparent

▶ It saves time when amendment proves necessary, since cause-and-effect phenomena become clearer in the logigram.

In other words, why be complicated when we can be simple?

Annex 2: Economic

Quality cost in small & medium size companies

The results of diagnosing quality in small and medium size companies clearly show, whatever the size of the company, preventative efforts directly contribute to reducing costs. (The study upon which the data for this annex is based has been collected primarily from the manufacturing sector. To date shipping data is not yet available, but some of the lessons can be transferred from the information which we have.)

Quality must be measured in order to assess the performance of a company. Quality cost is one of the ways to measure this. A quality cost system does two things: it allows for the identification and cost of the expenditure made to prevent non-conformities and errors; and it reveals loopholes and problems that prevent a company from attaining the necessary performance and competitiveness.

The quality cost concept is not an innovation. It is much argued about, and is misunderstood in most companies. There is contention between those concerned with quality costs and those who emphasise 'non-quality' costings.

Today, it is necessary to extend these two concepts. It is not sufficient any more to assess only the costs attributable to such things as the quality department, operations, rework, scrap, repairs, and claims. Management errors must, in the same way, be incorporated into the global costings. All these elements are opportunities which can be taken hold of and turned into profit.

Methodology

To get an idea of the range of things having an effect on the company's quality performance, we can examine and highlight the results obtained through a 'quality diagnostic' of small and medium size companies. From the 113 diagnoses completed, 54 were selected as being significant. Many of the other companies could not be included in this study because most of them do not operate an appropriate accounting system (as far as quality cost data acquisition was concerned). In other companies, the error margins relating to the most important costs would have jeopardised the credibility of this analysis and were therefore not acceptable.

The data acquired and used was selected by a team that included the company's staff and two quality engineers. A diagnosis lasts three to seven days depending on the size of the company. Such an approach allows for most of the staff involved in various functions of the company to understand the procedures and gives them sufficient time to collect the information needed for the study.

Quality concerns an attitude of mind based on communication and understanding, not on improvisation. It therefore takes time and patience.

The factors selected for this study were numerous but they conformed to the principles of modern quality management, ie: they satisfied a need, on time, and at the lowest possible cost. These factors were classified as:

■ Prevention cost

■ Appraisal cost

■ Failure cost

Prevention cost represents the deliberate investment that a company makes to prevent non-conformities and errors. Prevention cost is the very foundation of quality. Sufficient time must be allocated to defining the product or service, the objectives, and the means necessary to control quality standards.

Prevention cost incorporates the following: administration of the quality function; design, planning and verification of the systems; preventive maintenance of the equipment; review and up-dating of instructions, specifications and procedures; surveys related to service warranty; quality improvement programme, and personnel training.

Appraisal cost represents an investment that may or may not have been made freely by a company. The company may decide on its own to control the quality of its activities or a system of control may be imposed upon it by major clients. Depending on the company, such control may be centralised or decentralised.

Appraisal cost incorporates the following: appraisal during the development of the equipment; new materials; methods and processes; inspections performed by the company's quality department; equipment, supplies,

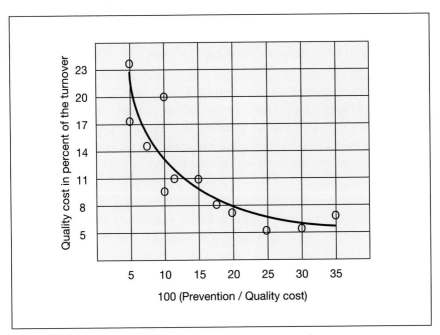

Figure B1 Effect of prevention on quality cost

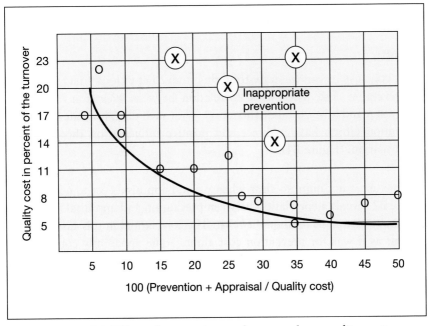

Figure B2 Effect of prevention and approval on quality cost

samples and premises necessary for the performance of inspections and tests; verification by external laboratories or organisations; operator's self-inspection, and evaluation of competitors products.

Failure cost represents an unintentional loss that is very concealed. Compared to the two other types of costs, failure includes a set of factors that are sometimes difficult to assign value to. If a company does not appreciate the extent of such costs, it may limit or even preclude the possibility of taking the corrective actions necessary to improve its performance.

Failure cost incorporates the following: losses included in standard costs; production losses and extra consumption of materials; losses on stock and inventory variance; material failures; lost sales and penalties; disputes and visits to customers; rework, and repairs; disposition of scrap; inventory of defective and obsolete items; excess inventory; under-used and standby equipment; losses of manpower efficiency, and insurance for product liability.

The sample used as a basis for this annex – 54 firms – does not reflect the situation in industry as a whole. It covers some small and medium size companies which have accepted the idea that a quality diagnostic could give them insight into ways to improve their performance and competitiveness.

Results

What conclusions can we draw from this study? Let us look first at the effect of prevention cost. There is a correlation between greater investment in prevention and lower total quality costs. With such data, it is safe to say that prevention efforts have a direct and positive influence on the company's profit margin. (Figure B1).

The picture is not quite so clear when we add appraisal cost to our analysis. Figure B2 reveals a correlation between prevention and appraisal investment and the reduction of total quality cost. The correlation, in this case, is not as evident as it was for prevention cost alone. Some apparently contradictory situations show up. If we analyse these situations, the following points emerge:

▶ The situations involve companies that have detailed inspection systems, generally covering final inspection with very little in-process inspection, ie: a costly inspection scheme.

Prevention efforts and corrective actions oriented toward prevention are rare or non-existent. Considering these factors, it is reasonable to think that both prevention and appraisal efforts are necessary to reduce quality costs. Nonetheless, we must keep in mind that appraisal or inspection effort, without appropriate investment in prevention, may lead to a feeling of false security and may generate unnecessary costs.

In order to compare and to assess problems and organisational loopholes in companies of different sizes, the firms were classified in terms of number of employees. For each class, the cost of failures per year was computed per person, for constant turnover. The correlation is outstanding: quality cost decreases dramatically with the size of the companies.

Two causes seem likely to account for this result:

▶ Larger companies are better organised. For instance, they probably have an engineering department or a quality department

▶ The cost of errors is spread over a larger sales turnover.

We also analysed the effect of prevention on companies of different sizes. It also highlights the fact that, whatever the size of the company, prevention efforts directly contribute to reducing quality cost.

It is quite obvious from this study that investment in both prevention and appraisal are necessary to reduce quality costs. But, investing exclusively in appraisal is a mistake that may lead to unacceptable costs. The protection it affords to the company's reputation is a fragile shield, as it can take a large bight out of the profit margin necessary to survive, develop, and compete.

Figures related to quality costs are a useful performance indicator for a company's executive. This study leads to the conclusion that, whatever the size of the company, quality directly contributes to the profit margin.

It is a safe investment: better prevention than cure.

Annex 3: People

How should we reward managers?

This contribution is the result of a study I performed in large French companies at the management level. The objective was to identify the expectations of managers with respect to being rewarded for their results accomplished within the framework of a quality system.

Should we reward managers? This is a question which is generally not discussed as it assumed that any manager is paid to take on his responsibilities. Yet in every programme of Total Quality Management it is necessary to recognise those who participate and play an important role in the improvement of quality.

■ This idea is based on two principles:

■ The reward is naturally expected as part of a relationship – winner to winner

Whatever effort the manager makes, he awaits a reward in recognition of this effort.

Managers are the persons who apply those principles in their private and business life as well as in their daily relations with their hierarchy and the people they have to manage and to mobilise towards desired aims necessary to expand the company

■ Is it true? Does the manager really need this reward? and if it's true, how?

■ Are the expectations different between managers depending on their rank in the company?

This is what I have tried to discover.

In order to answer the questions, we interviewed ten executives in charge of human resources in 10 major companies, and 124 managers from private and public companies.

Methodology

The methodology used to carry out this study can be divided into three parts:

▶ A list of questions designed to measure the importance given by managers in recognition of their performance,

▶ a list of possibilities for recognition by managers to be ranked in order of priority eg:

A. Progression in the company
B. Gratification through a monetary reward
C. Recognition through a gift
D. Enjoyment of life
E. Celebration of success
F. Recognition by hierarchy
G. Recognition by peers consideration
H. Improvement of skills.

▶ a list of specific rewards, from which to select and identify the most and the least significant ones.

A1. Change of function in the same department
A2. Promotion in the same department
A3. Transfer to another department with the same responsibilities
A4. Promotion and transfer to another department

B1. Bonus based in the company result
B2. Team bonus based on team achievements
B3. Individual bonus based on personal results
B4. Salary rise based on personal results

C1. Practical gifts
C2. Decorative gifts
C3. Temporary use of a car, country cottage etc

D1. A gastronomic dinner
D2. A holiday

E1. Happy hour and presentation of certificate
E2. Lunch or dinner with presentation of results
E3. A night of trophies for everyone recognised

E4. Annual party with colleagues and family

F1. Congratulations by top executive
F2. Presentation of results to top executive
F3. Letter of congratulation from the chairman
F4. Consultation about a new project

G1. Citation in company journal
G2. Results published on notice-board
G3. Membership of a company club
G4. Participation in managing business department

H1. Choice of a training course
H2. Participation in an external professional symposium
H3. Participation in an internal company seminar
H4. Sabbatical leave

Human resource executives

It was quite difficult to make these people speak about this subject.

Ten executives were willing to answer our questions:
6 in the public sector
4 in the private sector representing major companies.

100 per cent of them think that it is necessary to recognise managers for their results as it is a vital motivator for everybody.

70 per cent of them consider that the recognition of results should be recognised by something different from a reward. Indeed the word 'reward' suggests a medal or a prize just like at school.

In the first part of this study, a few executives mentioned that a promotion is more favoured than a simple reward. Occasionally a reward can be given but if the effort is made continuously, the manager has to be recognised by something different.

The word 'reward' is taken in a very restrictive sense. For example: according to an executive the choice of a training course was a form of recognition in itself.

As for an another executive, training was not considered a reward, it was a requirement for improving skills.

Nevertheless 40 per cent of them thought that rewards had to be intrinsic and extrinsic.

If the reward was to be considered as a form of recognition:

90 per cent of them agreed that it was necessary to reward managers according to the achievement of objectives.

80 per cent of them considered that the result obtained is more important than the attained target and should be the starting point for encouragement.

40 per cent of them mentioned that the reward should be given on an individual and collective basis, taking into account the value of teamwork.

80 per cent of them associated the value of the reward to the results obtained and not to a precise objective.

The notion of results was generally more important than the attained target. Human resources executives agreed on the necessity to recognise managers for their results and to value their performance.

The second part of this study informs us about the nature of rewards which may be considered as a means of recognising managers for their performances.

The best rewards for a manager were considered to be: the possibility of choosing a professional training course; then promotion and transfer to another department; a bonus based on meeting the team's objectives; and finally participation in the decisions of his department.

Managers

It was easier to question managers during quality management seminars.

124 have answered our questions, among them 36 senior managers.

99 per cent of them thought that they had to be recognised for their results. They agreed with human resource executives' opinion.

84 per cent of them considered that their results should be recognised by means of a reward. Only 40 per cent of them thought that the reward should be given differently. The word 'reward' related more to the word 'medal' for human resources executives than for managers.

68 per cent of them believed that rewards should be intrinsic and extrinsic. 64 per cent of them dismissed the extrinsic reward only if they did not have a deep feeling of participation. In that case the extrinsic reward turned out to be of little value.

75 per cent of them estimated that it was necessary to reward managers according to the objectives attained and 61 per cent of them thought that it was important to encourage the staff's participation.

68 per cent of them preferred receiving a team reward rather than an individual one. The team's spirit as well as the notion of meeting targets were quite strong for managers.

79 per cent associated the importance of the rewards to the objective attained and not to the result. The manager's answer was the opposite to that given by human resources executives.

This indicates significant variations between the answers from managers and human resources executives. Was it a communication problem or a misunderstanding of manager's wishes? Or again did the restraints of human resources executives in managing people on a day to day basis not allow them to express freely their points of view?

The second part of this study reveals what would be the three best forms of recognition for managers:

A. Promotion
B. Recognition
C. Skills improvement

The third part of this study informed us about managers' wishes concerning rewards. They considered that the best rewards were a holiday and participation in their department's decisions.

The study also showed that many managers complain about the fact that they do not really participate in their department's decisions. Most of the time they only executive orders coming from a higher level. The feel like pawns on a chessboard. In third and fourth positions, managers mentioned promotion in their own department and the desire to be consulted about new projects concerning the company.

Here again the vision of human resources executives compared with manager's wishes shows important differences.

Senior managers versus middle managers

Is there a difference concerning recognition and the nature of rewards between senior managers and middle managers?

In order to answer this question, we compared managers' answers from the same company. The sample was composed of:

12 senior managers

88 middle managers

Senior managers considered that the three best forms of recognition for a manager were:

F. Consideration by position (status)
B. Recognition
G. Consideration by peers

Middle managers consider that the three best forms of recognition for a manager are:

B. Recognition by reward
A. Promotion
H. Skills improvement

Senior managers position their needs for recognition on the highest side of the scale of individual needs.

Middle managers demonstrated their needs for recognition at a lower level on the same scale. But they hoped to accede to higher levels of responsibilities once their competences were recognised, and they were ready for promotion.

For all managers, the results as a whole were similar in terms of status.

The third part of the study allowed us to explore wishes in terms of rewards.

Senior managers considered that the five best rewards were: salary increase based on personal results, participation in their department's decisions, a holiday, promotion with transfer and finally a lunch in recognition of results.

As for middle managers, they considered that the five best rewards were: a holiday, participation in their department's decisions, internal promotion, the choice of a professional training course and finally the opportunity to start a new project.

Senior and middle managers' views, except for the holiday and participation in their department's decisions; were different.

Middle managers thought that payment is a form of recognition but it was not retained as a reward in their top priorities. They wanted to participate in decisions and to be consulted.

They wished to be promoted in the same department and to be transferred if it was the only way to obtain that promotion.

They wished to have the right to choose their training course, and if it was not possible, well, why not choose a holiday which would enable them to dream about some other things, far away from work?

Senior manager preferred a salary rise based on their personal results and a promotion with transfer. They valued the social aspect of recognition through an event which could be celebrated all together.

Conclusion
The analysis of this study reveals that each manager feels the need to be recognised for their skills, his achievements and their ambitions.

This recognition should be a valued reward which they can share with their team.

Most rewards quoted by senior and middle managers concern: participation in their department's decision, promotion in the same department or with transfer, presentation of results during a lunch with the whole department's staff, the possibility of choosing a professional training course and why not a nice trip?

Except for those common choices, there were striking differences in the points of view between senior and middle managers.

Senior managers considered that a salary rise based on their results was the first motivation. Middle managers do not mention that reward in their 10 first choices. They only considered (in position 9) this type of recognition as a team bonus, when the objectives were achieved.

Another important difference was the wish expressed by middle managers to be consulted about the new projects concerning company activities. The idea was not mentioned among the 10 priorities chosen by senior managers.

Finally the notion of being congratulated by top management retained by senior managers seemed out of fashion for middle managers who wished above all to participate in decisions and to be consulted about new products.

A relevant point in this study was the fact that the differences between senior and middle managers were all the more significant when compared to the results obtained from human resources executives.

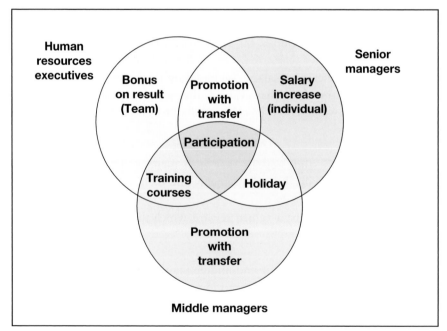

Figure C1 Participation is an uncommon expectation

The results of our study show that problems exist among executives and managers. It is necessary to admit it and to find solutions.

Among possible solutions we could consider the following ideas (Figure C1).

1. Favour internal promotion when it is possible, and if not consider a promotion through a transfer.

2. Encourage the participation of every manager in their department's decisions, and consult them before launching a new project, especially those who are directly affected by that change.

3. Give priority to the training of the managers who ask for it without imposing any course unless the necessity of it has been explained to them.

4. Grant a bonus based on significant results to a team and not to an individual.

5. Create a special occasion to provide an exceptional reward to crown a major success, but remember that it must be special.

6. Do not fall into the trap giving salary rises based on a short-term results. Everyone needs a decent salary, it is a basic factor and not a motivating one.

Finally we can conclude that a reward must reflect the pleasure and satisfaction arising from an action which is enjoyed more strongly than the effort required to accomplish it.

THE NAUTICAL INSTITUTE

Shipping Management Series

The efficient operation of ships requires a high level of management skill. Shipping is a service industry and it is essential that it meets customer demands. Their requirements imply that the cargo will be loaded, carried and delivered in good order and condition and that the ship proceeds in a safe, timely and reliable way.

It is a fact that major disasters capture the headlines and influence public opinion, groundings, strandings, collisions, fires and explosions have become the driving force for new legislation and the focus of new safety training standards emanating from the IMO.

Some of the IMO training requirements are linked to safe ship operations like the new ISM Code and the courses on human resources under the STCW 95 Convention, but in general shipping management is excluded and the skills which go with it have to be provided by industry. To support industry in this endeavour the Council of The Nautical Institute has commissioned a series of training books and a video covering: *Command; Watchkeeping Safety and Cargo Management in Port; Commercial Management for Shipmasters; The Management Diploma Scheme; Managing Safety and Quality in Shipping, a guide to ISM, ISO 9002 and TQM and The Mariner's Role in Collecting Evidence,* Video and Book.

Command:– This is a major reference work covering all aspects of command at sea and is divided with six sections covering; Advice to new masters; Command law, commerce and training; Propulsion, control, communications, catering and maintenance; Navigation, seamanship and shiphandling; Case histories. It can be linked to a study programme for senior officers aspiring to command.

Watchkeeping Safety and Cargo Management in Port (Sponsored by the UK P&I Club) by Captain P. Roberts:- covers, Watchkeeping duties; Arrival; Mooring; Safety in Port; Taking over the watch; Commercial documentation; Break bulk cargo operations; Specialist dry bulk operations; Tanker operations; Ballast operations; Stress and stability; Cargo condition; Cargo quality; Ships Services; Pollution prevention; Ship's security; Securing the cargo; Keeping records; Departure and comprehensive appendices. The book is aimed at junior watchkeeping officers.

Commercial Management for Shipmasters (Sponsored by the UK P&I Club) by Mr R.L. Tallack:– covers, Contractual and management relationships between owner and master; Practical management techniques to be used on board; Budgets and management information systems; Terms of trade and bills of lading; Legal framework for contracts of carriage; Charter parties, the master's role as manager; Marine insurance; Contracts for purchasing supplies and services; Managing a technical cost centre; A changing approach to safety; Commercial perspectives on emergencies; Renewal, sale purchase and financing supported by comprehensive appendices. The book is aimed at shipmasters and fleet managers.

The Mariner's Role in Collecting Evidence – book and video cover:
Cargo Damage Loss, and Shortage; Insurance Damage; Under Performance and Over Consumption Claims; Bunker Disputes; Unsafe Berths and Ports; Damage to Fixed and Floating Objects; Pollution; General Average; Salvage; Collisions; Labour Disputes and Displinary Procedures; Personal Injury; Stowaways; Refugees

The Management Diploma Scheme:– The Institute offers by distance learning, a series of modules aimed at improving personal effectiveness. The modules cover:– Setting objectives and planning; Controlling; Solving problems and making decisions; Leading and motivating staff; Delegating; Managing time; Running effective meetings; Coaching others.

For further information contact:
The Publications Officer, The Nautical Institute, 202 Lambeth Road, London, SE1 7LQ, Tel: 020 7928 1351 Fax 020 7401 2817

Other sources of information:
The International Maritime Organisation, 4 Albert Embankment, London SE1 7SR; Tel 0171 735 7611; Fax: 0171 587 3210

Publications catalogue, including ISM Code

International Chamber of Shipping/International Shipping Federation, 12 Carthusian Street, London EC1M 6EB; Tel: 0171 417 8844; Fax: 0171 417 8877

Guidelines on ISM Code application

The Institute of Quality Management, 61 Southwark Street, London SE1 1SB; Tel: 0171 401 7227; Fax 0171 401 2725

Monthly journal: Quality World

Auditor registration, books and library

The British Standards Institution, 389 Chiswick High Road, London W4 4AL; Tel: 0181 996 7000; Fax: 0181 996 7001
Publishes ISO standards

Monthly journal: British Standards

Catalogue of British and international standards